SNOWY EARTH
COMES GLIDING
by Evelyn Eaton

DRACO FOUNDATION
STAR ROUTE 1, BOX 76
INDEPENDENCE, CALIFORNIA 93526

CONTENTS

Illustrations

Author's Notes

I HAVE TO THANK the Marsden Foundation and its Director, Dr. Elizabeth Bonbright, for two generous grants and much encouragement to undertake the long and difficult research required for this book.

I have also to thank the Chapelbrook Foundation for a generous grant-in-aid toward the project.

Above all I have to thank Paiute, Washo, and Arapaho friends, especially those who travel the Indian Way, for their courtesy and their help.

I would like to stress that at no time, under no circumstances, has any Indian given me any information about the Ghost Dance, or acknowledged its existence. The songs and accounts of the Ghost Dance in this book are taken from contemporary records of those who had their information directly from Wovoka or those in contact with him before his death in 1932.

EVELYN EATON

Acknowledgments

The poems *Charm for going hunting*, and *Morning Prayer*, by Mary Austin, are taken from her book *Children Sing in the Far West*, and are reprinted by permission of the publisher, Houghton Mifflin, Company.

The poem "Yet also we keep the seasons of the sheep," by Gordon Grant, is taken from *The Shaman at Ending* and reprinted by permission of the author.

The songs from the Ghost Dance are taken from the 14th Annual Report of the Bureau of Ethnology, J. W. Powell, to the Secretary of the Smithsonian Institution, for 1892-93, and reprinted by permission.

Photograph on page 10 is by Ron Powell, and photographs on pages 38, 44, and 86 are by Phil Pister, both courtesy of the California Department of Fish and Game. Photograph on page 72 is by Curt Phillips, and on pages 6 and 78 by Enid Larson. All other photographs are by Bill and Louise Kelsey.

Wùmbí' ndomä'n, Wûmbí' ndoma'n,
Wûmbí' ndomä'n, Wûmbí' ndoma'n,
Nuvä rí' p noyo' wanä, Nuvä' ri'p noyo'wanä,
Nuvä rí' p noyo' wanä, Nuvä' ri'p noyo'wanä.

The Whirlwind!   The Whirlwind!
The Whirlwind!   The Whirlwind!
The snowy earth comes gliding, the snowy earth comes gliding.
The snowy earth comes gliding, the snowy earth comes gliding.

SONG FROM THE PAIUTE GHOST DANCE, referring to the coming of a new world, a new age, when evil will be destroyed and good ways return with peace and happiness. The new world is represented as white with snow, advancing swiftly, driven by a whirlwind.

PART ONE

I

I HAVE LIVED IN THIS REGION now for thirteen years, up and down what Mary Austin called The Land of Little Rain, and the Indians called the Country of Lost Borders, which the white men named the Owens Valley, and the official guide book describes as "America's Deepest Valley," between the Sierra Nevada's alpine crest and the Inyo-White Mountains in Eastern California.

For ten of those thirteen years I have been drawn into the Paiute way of life, accepted in the Sweat Lodges and Ceremonies as a sick white woman who came there for help and healing, and later, to my joy, as a friend. I think a trusted friend.

At first there were many who resented this intrusion of any white into Indian privacy. One man, I remember, could not resist coming close to me to say bitter things about whites where I must hear them. It was a surprise, and I felt a surge of glad pride to overhear him, not long ago, explaining to a visiting brother who had obviously asked "What's that white woman doing here?"

"She's one of us. She's *Paiute!*"

Last year, after a shared experience, an older woman who had kept aloof from the beginning, whispered, "Now it has opened up for you. It didn't take too long. Now you are really Indian."

It is in gratitude to Paiute, Washo, Shoshone, and Arapaho friends that I offer this book, in the hope that it may "open up" the minds of others to the dignity, the stature, the wisdom, of a proud and patient people, the Indians of Owens Valley.

Also I hope this primer will introduce others, among them the young, the eager, the spiritually hungry, to their heritage of wisdom. There was never any need for those who live in the Americas to turn to the East, to India, for enlightenment. The ancient wisdom is here, the wisdom of the occident, *Amerind* Mandalas and symbols, the Medicine Wheel, the Four Directions, the Thunder

*Where ancient peoples left the witness of their
lives, their visions, the strength of their faith for
us to ponder.*

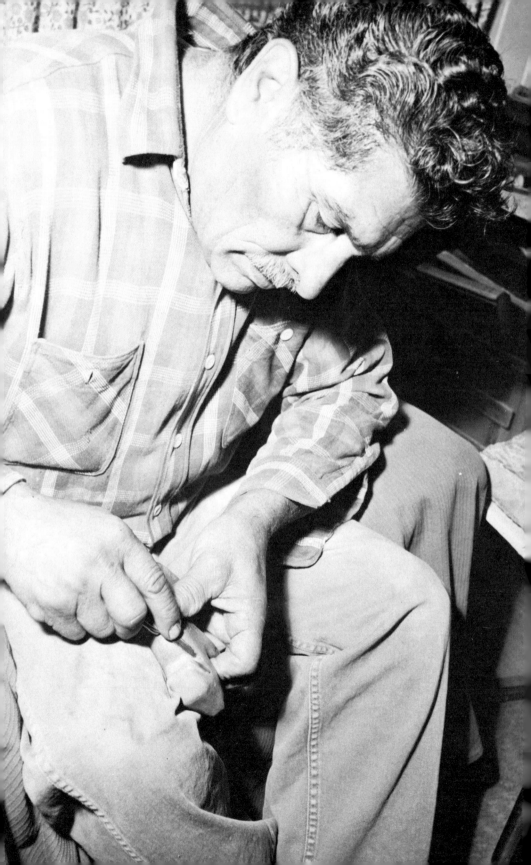

Bird, Shaman with the Medicine Bag, Ritual Dancers, Big Horn Sheep . . . here in the desert, and on the towering ranges flanking it.

The greatest concentration of hieroglyphic symbols is in the Coso Range, west of Death Valley, east of the Sierra and south of Owens Lake.

Coso Range rises about 6,000 feet into the piñon-juniper zone where there were abundant food resources, and descends to semi-desert valleys, where during the pluvial period at the end of the Ice Age there were four great inland lakes, now salt flats.

For ten thousand years it has preserved traces of ancient civilizations, and for four thousand years an extraordinary collection of prehistoric rock pictures, the most extensive in the New World, as interesting, as beautiful, vital and full of joy and purpose as those in the Lascaux caves in France, the Rhodesian Rock engravings, and other rediscovered places where ancient peoples left the witness of their lives, their visions, the strength of their faith for us to ponder.

Nowadays we need a four-wheel drive — (and the Navy's permission) to travel Coso Range.

Why the Navy, in the middle of the desert, several hundred miles from any sea? Since 1943 The Naval Weapons Center, based at China Lake, has taken over twelve-hundred square miles for missile testing, and closed the area to the public, also to the Indians who used to come to the Coso Hot Springs to worship the Great Spirit and take the healing waters He put there for their use.

As Raymond Stone, Paiute sculptor and pipe-maker for his people, put it, when he acted as spokesman for a group which journeyed to Coso Hot Springs in November 1971, to meet with government officials and other authorities, to discuss the situation and set forth the Indian point of view:

"This land that I talk about is one of our sources of religion. Our people years back used this land for healing. They came here and took the mud baths and drank the water that comes out of the hot springs, and as I look back from today to yesterday it must be a wonderful country in there, from what I can understand from

3

Raymond Stone, Paiute sculptor, at work on a
buffalo figure out of red catlinite (pipestone)
from which he makes the pipeheads for
his people.

some of the older people who travelled that place. It has something that the Great Spirit has set aside for the people to use, not to sell it, and not to abuse it in any way, but to go there and pray and use what is there for help on their way."

He shares with his people a dream, growing slowly to a hope, that sometime, in their lifetime, perhaps *soon*, a portion of their sacred ancestral lands at Coso Range may be restored to them for spiritual and healing purposes, that Coso Hot Springs may be re-opened for the use and benefit of all. When that happens, new life will flow through the valley and the blessing of the Great Spirit spread over the land Meanwhile they wait and work.

At first I was disturbed at the knowledge of missiles exploding in this sacred region, and all the debris of a testing ground strewn against the basalt cliffs where the ancient drawings are, and at the deprivation of the Indians, barred from their hot springs, but at least the Navy has protected the area from the vandalism and pollu-tion of the general tourist public. Guided groups of responsible people, scientists, students, and others who request permission, are allowed in at stated times, and there are back roads, faint trails, ways to go on foot to places not actually within the forbidden area, close enough to the past and protected from the present, where we may enter timeless solitude.

The edges of the sacred places are more and more encroached upon, but still, in 1973, the grandeur, the elbow room, the breath-ing space, the breathing itself, remain as they have been for thou-sands of years, free, and apparently unpolluted.

A few miles east, a few miles west, the beer cans, the trash, the noise, the careless greed . . . here the only signs of human passing delight the eye and lift the spirit. *Art* is here, records of the past, wistful messages, hopefully foreshadowing the future, pecked and painted outlines of Bighorn Sheep, Hunters, Medicine Men and Ritual Dancers, revealing something of the lives and the culture of the people who left them there.

Their physical existence must have depended largely on the huge Bighorn herds. There are many depictions of the hunt, men

5

Art is here, records of the past, wistful messages
foreshadowing the future.

with atlatls, men with bows, men with dogs, attacking the sheep, among more ritualistic figures with sheephorn headdresses, medicine bags, and groups of sacred dancers, in formation, doing a step easily recognizable where Indians still dance today.

> They are gone,
> the great herds,
> the hunters,
> the dancers,
> gone.
>
> Weathered shapes remain
> pecked into the rock.
>
> As long as rock endures
> as long as earth turns
> men and sheep will dance
> Horned ones dance
> here
> to Nu'mi/na'a.

There are also, in some places where the drawings are found, remains of blinds, and dummy hunters made of piled rocks perched on the edges of the cliffs, on the north or shady side of the canyons, where they would be seen from below in silhouette. John Muir says of stone blinds and dummy hunters:

"On the tops of nearly every one of the Nevada mountains I have visited I found small nestlike enclosures built of stones, in which I afterwards learned one or more Indians would lie in wait while their companions scoured the ridges below, knowing that the alarmed sheep would surely run to the summit, and when they could be made to approach with the wind, they were shot at short range.

"Great numbers of Indians were required, more than they could usually muster, counting in squaws, children and all; they were compelled therefore, to build rows of dummy hunters out of stones,

7

along the ridge tops which they wished to prevent the sheep from crossing."

Here and there these remain adding their testimony to the witness of the rock drawings.

The Bighorns were plentiful in those ancient days, now an almost vanished species on the endangered list. Still occasionally they show themselves far off on rocky crags and inaccessible places. I came upon a big ram once, at sunrise, silhouetted against the sky, high above Deep Springs Lake.

It was before I had seen the Rock Drawings at Coso, or knew about the "Grandfathers." The sight of the great ram with his curled horns and his majestic dignity, impressed me more than the startle of coming suddenly upon a rare wild beast. Though I was on the valley floor and he was on the mountain it was more than a distant glimpse, a greeting between "relatives," it was an Encounter. I stood staring upward until he disappeared, then I found that my breath was short and I was trembling.

Later I learned that the Bighorn occupied the sacred place given to the Buffalo by the tribes of the Great Plains. Both were the source of food, clothing, tools and ritual magic, as the Hare to the Algonquins, the Salmon and the Reindeer to Eskimos, the Beaver to the Micmacs, Moose, Wolves, Birds, Turtles and other animals to other tribes, the Eagle to everyone . . . great supernatural Beings, "Grandfathers," willing to give themselves, body and blood, to feed and sustain their people.

> YET ALSO we keep the seasons of the sheep
> moving into the desert
> toward perpetual summer
> the high-climbing ones
> with their horns curving
> towards those long dead
> long dust.
>
> Oh sky, we say, upstanding father,

9

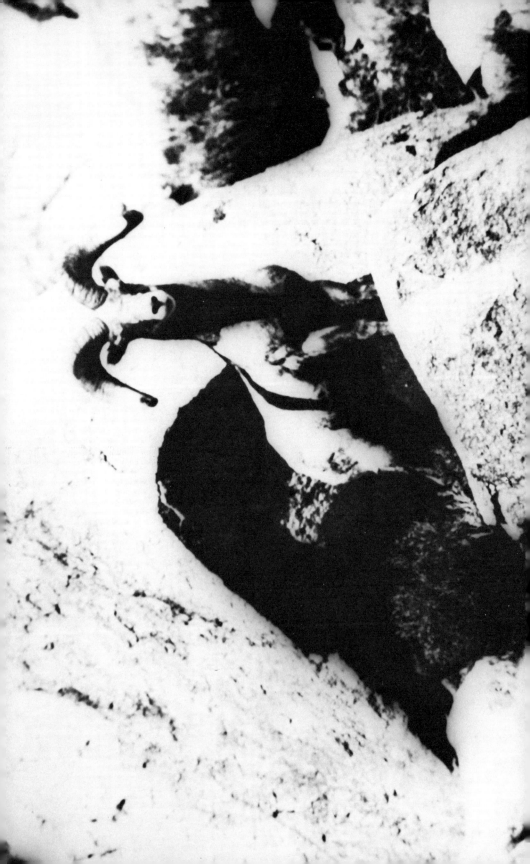

some speech must we offer;
this tight stone shall carry our voice.
And we harrow into it
the shapes of the spirit, the tall ones
whose heads shall mirror the great sun
at his clearest hour
upon our questions.

To this end
we have placed them in the high places,
watching
confronting the wind.

       —Gordon Grant from *The Shaman at Ending*.

"The high-climbing ones with their horns curving."

II

Coso is a Shoshonean word for *fire*, appropriate to the steaming hot springs, still bubbling up at 204°F. and to the volcanic lava formations scattered through the region. The Western Shoshoni and Paiutes of the Coso Range may or may not have been descendants of the people who made the rock drawings. All we know for sure is that they were living here when the white men came in 1860, and that archeologists believe they were there 2000 years ago.

Sidney M. Lamb in his *Linguistic Prehistory in the Great Basin* says they spoke a Shoshoni-Comanche dialect, one of the Numic Linguistic branches, and that this Shoshonean Paiute group was part of a Uto-Aztecan language family which included Hopi, Pima, and the Aztecs of Mexico. There are traces of Aztec influence in the valley to this day, for example on some of the basket designs and beadwork.

It is not important to us now whether the Western Shoshonis, the Paiutes, or an earlier group they may have displaced, left us this heritage. What matters are the drawings. Can we recover their meanings? In the light of modern research into other lost civilizations, can we decipher them and make them ours?

Here are vivid, joyful works of art, a delight, an end in themselves, but here are also, obviously, communications, urgent appeals, surviving thousands of years of erosion of wind and sand and climatic upheaval to reach our alien eyes, and we are in need of what they could tell us.

The interpretation usually given is that petroglyphs and pectographs were primitive forms of hunting magic which ignorant and superstitious people thought helped them to hunt down and kill the animals depicted. Dancers, ancient symbols and other designs were probably decorative, or may also have had something to do with the hunt.

"The high-climbing ones with their horns curving."
Coso petroglyph.

This is as wide of the mark as to imagine that the drawings of fish in the Roman Catacombs were put there by primitive tribes of fishermen, using the place for shelter, who drew the symbols to help them make an exceptional catch. Or that the lamb in churches was a form of superstitious magic in favor with primitive shepherds to help them increase their flocks. Or that Jason's Ram with the Golden Fleece was an agricultural symbol to improve the breed. Or that doves, halos, crosses, images of the saints, the angels and the Trinity, were merely decorative.

The Christian catechumen understood that the fish was a symbol representing the Master Jesus. Pagan enemies from whom it was carefully concealed, did not. In the same way the designs pecked into rock thousands of years ago may have a significant meaning carefully hidden from the uninitiated.

In most of the studies on Amerind artifacts one is apt to read statements like the following:

"When the first studies were made of the customs of the Indians in the area, the remnant population had no faintest memory of the rock drawings or sheep hunting ritual."*

"By the time the white man got around to asking about these rock drawings, not even the oldest Indian could give the slightest information — only that they had been done long ago by the ancients for an unknown purpose."

In the light of the wealth of traditional knowledge handed down among them in the Owens Valley, I think it more likely that the Indians both knew and could have told, but were not about to reveal their secrets to the enemy, whose avowed policy was to stamp out the Indian way.

Even among themselves, except at certain ceremonies, or on very safe occasions, the Indians do not talk of their sacred mysteries. It is unlikely that they would divulge them to the first curious white who came along. There is, in fact, a very deep resentment of writers, photographers, archeologists, and probers of all sorts who invade the reservations, though many books which could not have

*Rock Drawings of the Coso Range, Grant, Baird & Pringle.

been written without Indian help, such as the classic *Black Elk Speaks*,** show that those who approach in the spirit of humility, a desire to learn, and above all respect for the Amerind Mysteries will be guided and taught what they ask to know.

** *Black Elk Speaks*, John G. Neihardt.

III

IF THE PAINTINGS on the Coso Rocks were, as some authorities have pronounced them to be, merely to help on the hunt, there would have been more pictures of the animals most frequently hunted, the hare, the antelope, the prairie dog, the lizard, but there are very few among the thousands of depictions of sheep and other symbols pecked beside them, circles, crosses, ladders, medicine bags, ceremonial figures and dancers.

There are circles everywhere, the plain sphere, the sphere with a point in the center, which Freemasons will recognize, the sphere with spokes radiating upward, emblem of the rising sun, with spokes radiating downward, emblem of the setting sun, with spokes radiating outward in a complete circle, emblem of the sun at its meridian. There is the circle bisected by a cross, the circle starting from a spiral, the circle with hub and spokes like a wheel, the circle linked to other circles, an infinite variety of these basic designs, scattered from Coso through the Owens Valley, deep into Nevada.

The circle is the oldest, most universal symbol of Deity, from the stationary disc representing the Sun God, to the great turning Wheel of the Universe, representing both the Creator and the Created, where everything in the Cosmos finds its appointed place. This is the greatest of Amerindian Mandalas, corresponding to the Hindu Mandala which so interested Jung, and to which he frequently refers. (Mandala, the Hindu term for a circle, a *yantra*, the instrument or emblem in the form of a ritual geometric design used in meditation, not only in India, but increasingly in the West.)

The Mexican Great Calendar Stone, the Egyptian Lotus, the Alchemists' Flower of Gold, Dante's Mystical Rose, the Zodiacal Circle, the Round Table of the Arthurian Knights, and the Great Medicine Wheel of the Indians represent the same central truths.

17

Petroglyph, Coso Range.

They are all 'mandalas' sacred formulas for meditation, points of departure on the journey towards union with the Compassionate Finality, Numin'a'a, Wakan-tanka, Wakonda, the Great Holy, Flame of Life, the Great Spirit, the Creator under myriad names.

The circle is everywhere reflected in the Indian way of living, down to the physical details of everyday life. The encampment should be round, with the opening to the east, toward the rising sun, the dwelling place should be round, with the opening toward the east. It is a hardship to have to live in a government-built angular box, but as one woman has said, "I may have to live in a square house but I can still be a round house person." The Sweat Lodge is round, the hole in the center containing the fiery rocks is round, the sun is round, the world is round, the bird's nest is round, life is a round between birth and death, everything revolves in a circle, everything has its appointed place on the Wheel of the Universe. So also the community should be an enlargement of the family circle, living harmoniously in a round encampment. People thrive best when their surroundings mirror universal law. Buckminster Fuller's geodesic dome is no new concept, we are rediscovering the comfort, the rightness of the Paiute wickiup and the easily transported ti-pi of other tribes.

There are poignant references to the circle in *Black Elk Speaks*, John Neihardt's account of the talks he had with that great Medicine Man of the Oglala Sioux, and in many other written accounts of various tribes, but it is in the outward enacted symbolism of the ceremonies, the dances, the ritual of the pipe, and the Sweat Lodge that the teaching of the circle is so basically evident that it becomes second nature. It is today still everywhere presented to us in the round baskets, the round designs on them, the neckpieces, the medallions, with their infinite varieties of color and pattern. I have a medallion made for me by an Arapaho woman on the Wind River Reservation in Wyoming. It shows the four directions with the eightfold paths to the Center. It is very like the Chinese Yang-Yin, surrounded by the eight trigrams. The woman who made it said she got the colors, mauves, reds, purples, from the mountains out-

19

side her window, as they looked, after a storm, and the design from her husband, who "remembers knowing the old ways."

I have another, made for me by a Paiute friend, in the Owens Valley. It is blue and black and white, with the design of a sacred bird in the center. This friend also made me a necklet in the colors of the four old men, blue, white, red and turquoise. The neckband shows a symbolic design of a Lodge, with seated people, round a Medicine Man. The fall of the necklet, from neckband to forearm round the shoulders and breast, is an intricate design of paths towards the center. It is a very ancient pattern, and even the beads out of which it is made were taken from an older necklet, "My aunt made it, long time ago," it is at least a hundred years old, probably copied from an earlier design, handed down to the aunt.

There are some of these necklets, a specialty of the Paiute tribe, especially those from Pyramid Lake, in the Museum at Independence, but none more beautiful than those that are being made today in the Owens Valley.

IV

WHEN THE WHITES ARRIVED in the Coso region a little over a hundred years ago, they found Shoshoni living in the old rhythmic ways their ancestors had used for thousands of years, except that now the Bighorn Sheep were very scarce. They were not extinct, like the mastodon, the prehistoric elephant, camel and horse, which all lived in the region once and left their tracks and traces in the clay of dried up lakes. There were still a few sheep in rocky inaccessible places, but the great herds had long ago disappeared, driven out for reasons we can only guess at.

The invention of the bow may have been one, with its superiority over the atlatl as a hunting weapon, though the atlatl still appeared in the hands of warrior and shaman, as a symbol of power, like the sword and the mace long after their practical use was obsolete. The bow made hunting easier. A man no longer had to stand up and show himself to the quarry as he hurled his spear. He could shoot from ambush, he could be hidden behind a rock, he could kill more often than he missed.

But the major reason for the disappearance of the herds seems to have been climatic upheaval changing the country from a series of verdant, well-watered valleys with four great lakes, into an arid desert of salt flats and alkali wastes. The Bighorn went in search of better feeding grounds. Those who remained became exceedingly scarce. Some of the tribes followed the herds, joining ethnic groups in the north and the west. Those who stayed were a small number (there were about a hundred when the white man came) since the land could not support more under the changed conditions. They continued to hunt the rare sheep, the occasional deer or antelope, but mostly now they lived on smaller game, rabbits, wild fowl, fish, the larvae of some insects, greens, seeds, including mesquite, piñon nuts and berries.

The gathering of food was a communal affair, especially antelope and rabbit hunts, to which hunters came from as far as fifty miles. May was the time for antelope, the fall for rabbit drives. These were practical, secular occasions. Rarely on the sacred rocks is there a picture of a rabbit or a Shaman with rabbit ears. Though he might now be the chief source of meat and his skin of warmth and comfort, in rabbit-skin blankets and rabbit-skin clothes, the rabbit did not become the Grandfather. The Coso Grandfather was still the Bighorn Sheep, to whom Shaman and people prayed in the Sweat Lodges, and at the Sacred Ceremonies and Dances, and with whom the Shaman alone could talk directly of his people's needs.

V

Charm for Going Hunting
O my brothers of the wilderness,
My little brothers,
For my necessities
I am about to kill you!
May the Master of Life who made you
In the form of the quarry
That the children may be fed,
Speedily provide you
Another house;
So there may be peace
Between me and thy spirit.

—Mary Austin

THE INDIAN, with his instinctive, inborn art of living in friendly relationship with all life, hunts in a different manner from the white man. He learns as a child to consider the animals who share the earth with him as "relatives." He knows that he must kill them only when there is a need for food, for clothing, for himself, for his family, and for the people. He knows that he must first ask pardon of the animal he is to kill, must kill only one, the first that the Grandfathers show to him, and must kill it quickly as mercifully as possible.

First he must prepare himself by prayer, and sometimes fasting, for the hunt, and when he has killed he must give thanks to the Grandfathers and to the quarry. Then he must make sure that not a scrap is wasted, that all is shared, and he must not hunt again until there is a new need.

The Indian hunter, if he is following the Indian ways, does not put on fancy dress and take along a lot of booze, he does not hunt to *prove* anything, how good a shot he is, what an expensive gun he has, how many of his little brothers he can kill in a day. Such procedures, such thoughts even, make "the spirits" angry, and bring on a just punishment.

A Paiute friend of mine told me that when he was a young man he was very proud of his skill as a hunter. One day he went out after deer and came suddenly upwind into a clearing where there were four of them. Before he had time to think what he was doing he had killed all four. After the first moment of exhilaration, he began to be aghast. It was evening, getting dark, he was many miles from the reservation, and he would hardly be able to get the meat from the deer down the mountain, even if he could skin and cut them up as quickly and efficiently as he had killed them. He worked with all his skill and strength, and managed to stagger under the weight of three, but one would have to stay there, for the coyotes and buzzards to find and feast on. A fine grown buck, which could have made another good hunt and another good feast.

"I was sorry," he said. "I offered tobacco, but the spirits were angry. I heard a voice, the Old Man of that place. He said 'You will never see another deer.' I never did. I went on trying a year or two. I was young, I didn't believe, didn't want to believe. People tell me deer here, deer there. I go to see. Plenty signs, no deer. People see them, kill them, come back with their deer. I never see one. After awhile I know the Old Man speak true. I put my gun away. Twenty-seven years now I don't hunt. That is how it is."

"I'm sorry," I said.

He smiled. "I'm sorry too."

"I think I'm glad that you don't kill the deer or any animal."

He smiled again. His smile was a warmth I always waited for and loved to see.

"Hunting is good," he said, "if you don't take more than one. The first one the Grandfathers show you, that one you kill. Not proud, not talk how good you shoot. Be *thinking*. You bring meat, people eat, make mocassins, what they want. Talk to the Grandfathers, thank them, and the deer also. The deer get blessing, you get blessing, that way hunting good."

24

The Indian is the relative of the animals and plants who share the world with him. When an Indian boy gallops his horse without saddle or bridle, in perfect control and coordination, so that they move as one, it is because they share the knowledge a chief once revealed to J. Allen Boone (*Kinship With All Life*).

"The chief wants me to tell you," his interpreter said, "that for you to 'full-know' what you have asked him, you would have to be Indian born, Indian taught, and grow up with an Indian pony as your brother. Then you would understand the Great Mystery. You would be part of the Great Mystery. But he will tell you something about it in sign language and he says for you to catch what you can."

From the expressive signs, the 'catcher' understood that "Indian and pony were functioning as a single unit in mind, heart, body and purpose."

This oneness with all that live is the Indian heritage, though other sensitive people with compassionate vibrations, who breathe forth the fragrance of a holy life like Saint Francis, have it also from birth, or develop it through meditation and lives in harmony with the Great Mystery, the Big Holy.

It is in the rhythm of their approach, the way that they walk toward those who share the world with them; four-footed, two-footed, winged, are fellow-guests in the house of the Great Spirit, with an equal right to be there, an equal importance in the scheme of things, their place on the Great Medicine Wheel. The interdependence of created things is a concept slowly beginning to be understood. It does not have to be explained to Indians, to those who follow the Indian way.

VI

BESIDES the symbolism of the sacrificial lamb, sheep have a universal symbolism. Aries, the Ram, is the first sign of the Zodiac, the beginning of a cycle, the start of the immortal quest, which was also symbolized by the Golden Fleece to be taken from a great Ram.

In Egypt the Ram was the symbol of the Egyptian Zeus, Amon-Re, "King of the Gods," who is always shown wearing Ram's Horns.

The horns themselves in the Egyptian system of hieroglyphs meant "what is above the head" and "to open up a path for oneself." They were also associated with music, the lyre being shaped like two horns with the sound coming from between them.

Some tribes, for example, the Iroquois, have horn rattles, played by hitting the rattle against the palm of an open left hand, or on the left thigh, or twisted in a small circle above the hand, alone or with the water drum.

There are striking similarities between the ancient Egyptians and the Amerindians . . . the use of the feather, hieroglyphs, similar concepts of the Cosmos and of man's place in the universe. . . . If an Egyptian from the Middle Kingdom had arrived at Coso when the Rock Drawings were being made, he would have recognized Grandfather Big Horn Sheep as one of the gods, representing Maat, the Truth, the Divine Order established at the creation of the universe, the essence of existence. To follow Maat was to live in harmony with the highest good.

"In its personal application the good life was living in attunement with Maat, exemplified in the self discipline of the 'silent man' who is always patient, calm and self-effacing, master of his impulse, 'striving after every excellence until there is no fault in his nature.' " This was also the Chinese conception of Tao, the path that lay at the heart of all existence and the order of the universe.

27

There are striking similarities between the ancient Egyptians and the Amerindians. Bas relief by Raymond Stone.

The virtues which both the Egyptians and the Chinese extolled and sought after were honesty, truthfulness, justice, generosity and frankness. These are also Indian concepts, especially the example of the silent man. Indians not only value silence, and recommend it in stories and pointed sayings. . . . "Listen, or your tongue will make you deaf," "No flies come into a closed mouth," and a clause in an Indian prayer, "Oh my Grandfather, may I lose no good opportunity to hold my tongue." They feel comfortable in silence, and are often irritated, or at best amused, by the white man's "windmill machine" of constant chatter.

Silence, 'going behind the blanket,' removing oneself from useless or annoying contact are highly developed techniques, second nature to those who follow the Indian way, useful, one might say indispensable, at long boring meetings or other encounters with officialdom.

I remember once I came to the wrong house when I was looking for an Indian friend. Through the open doorway I could see a spry old lady cross the room to sink into a chair. In the moment that it took me to reach the doorstep she had "gone behind the blanket." There was a figure in the chair, yes, an ancient statue, it might have been of wood or clay, immobile, neither seeing nor hearing, and I could see no sign of breathing.

I stood politely in the opening, waiting for what my grandfather's people* call the "upchelase," the welcome, the permission for a stranger to enter, without which no well-bred person crosses a threshold. Then since I needed to know where my friend's house was I asked the image humbly, from where I stood, to please direct me — no flicker of a sign of life from what a few moments before had been a responsive and very agile human being. She sat "in a sacred manner," her human envelope beautiful to see, with the especial beauty of extreme old age, but that was all there was, a human envelope, without the animating spirit within.

Trouble had come to her door, in the shape of a strange white woman, whom she did not know and did not care to know, therefore she had gone away. I stayed awhile, in my ignorance, thinking

*The Micmacs and Malisites of Nova Scotia.

29

Thunderbird, with lighting from his wings, and
above his head the sign (circle) of the Great Spirit
and the Four Old Men, the Four Directions.
A Raymond Stone carving.

that she might come back, knowing my own harmless good intent, unwilling to see myself as she had seen me. I murmured soft apologies. I mentioned my friend's name. I sent thought-waves of respect to the wisdom-wrinkled face with the half-open, averted eyes.

Then I too went away, not behind the blanket, to fly with the wild geese, or ride the winds, or visit the Grandfathers — just prosaically, abashed and a little troubled, asking for guidance to where I needed to go. I had not taken ten steps before two children ran up to me, brother and sister, nine and ten. They ranged alongside, apparently expecting me just there and then, and we walked in companionable silence to their grandmother's house, up the hill, out of sight of the other house that I was leaving.

As soon as I arrived and as she drew me in, my Paiute friend said apologetically:

"She is a very old lady and does not like to be surprised."

"I did not mean to surprise her."

"I know."

I had learned enough not to ask her how she knew, and why she expected me that afternoon, when I had not planned, as I set out, that I would be coming to her. No more was said.

We sat down at the table strewn with beads and pieces of buckskin. She was making a cradleboard for some lucky baby. Her cradleboards are famous in the valley, so are her medallions and neckpieces. I turned over the finished and half finished work, wondering why, among the Eagles, and the Great Medicine Wheels, the ladders and loops and squares like those I had seen pecked into the Coso Rocks, there was no image of a Bighorn Sheep. She told me, without my having to ask, "Bighorn is not Paiute. Never Paiute. Belongs to some other people."

I asked her about the four colors she was working with.

"Always that way," she said. "For the Four . . ." she hesitated.

"The Four Directions?"

"Something."

I understood that 'directions" was not quite the word to be used, or else there should have been something added. More probably

3 1

this was not "when the time is right" for talking of these things. We smiled at one another and went into a companionable silence.

Each knew that we were thinking of the Four Old Men, the Sacred Four Great Primary Forces, the four servants of the Great Mysterious, who dwell at the four directions, East, South, West and North and watch over the four quarters of the universe. The Morning Star is the messenger of the Four Old Men, who are sometimes referred to as the Thunderbird, who watches the earth. They are also Summer, Winter, Day and Night, and in another grouping, the Wind, the Thunderers, the Sun and the Moon. The Pueblo Indians of Arizona and New Mexico call them simply "Those Above."

These four Great Ones have their appropriate colors, which vary a little from tribe to tribe, but they are usually black or dark blue, red, yellow and white, and these are also the colors of the four elements of life, the four courses, the four divides. They are everpresent, the sacred watchers, who guard the people from harm, the Protectors.

The cross is one of their symbols, the most universally depicted, so that when we see a circle or a sun-wheel with the cross inside it, or bisecting it, with four projections, we have the emblem of the Creator and his four Creative Forces. One legend says that the Four Old Men were commanded by the Great Spirit to create the universe, and when they finished their work they were given charge of it.

Suddenly I found myself looking down at the new pattern growing on the cradleboard my friend was beading. It was a cross within a wheel, like those I had seen at Coso, among the circles and stars and ladders, the dancers and the Bighorn Sheep.

But images of Bighorn Sheep dwindle north of Coso Range, and fade out altogether in the Owens Valley, where the Paiutes settled. Many of the other symbols, pecked into the rocks at Coso, remain and increase at places scattered northward, through the valley, but Bighorn Sheep is not a part of Paiute culture.

The Paiute Grandfathers have wings.

33

The Paiute grandfathers have wings. Eagle, red catlinite figure carved by Raymond Stone.

VII

THERE ARE MANY BIRDS in Amerindian mythology, as there are in other traditions.

Birds, according to Jung, in his *Symbols of Transformation* and *Psychology and Alchemy* are "beneficent animals representing spirits or angels, supernatural aid, thoughts and flights of fancy."

Hindu tradition considers birds to represent the higher states of being, symbolic of the soul. Egyptian tradition gave the bird a human head and the hieroglyph *Ba*, the soul. Loeffler-Delachaux, in his *Le Symbolism des contes de Fées* says that birds are universally recognized as intelligent collaborators with human beings in myths and folktales and that they are derived from the great bird-demiurges of the primitives — bearers of celestial messages and creators of the nether world.

The giant bird is always symbolic of a creative deity. Vedic tradition depicts the sun in the form of a huge bird, an eagle or a swan. Scandinavian myths refer to a gigantic bird called Hraesvelg which creates the wind by beating its wings. In North America there is the Thunder Bird, whose flapping wings make the sound of thunder and whose flashing eyes send forth the lightning. The Thunderbird nests on a high mountain or the top of unscalable rocky cliffs.

In the Ghost Dance, which originated among the Paiutes, the dancers wear Thunderbirds on their shirts, and sometimes a replica of him on their heads, cut from rawhide ornamented with beads. In the Arapaho version of the Ghost Dance there are songs referring to the Thunderbird.

Three of the best known are *Eyehé A' nie' sa na,' Ninaá niahu' na*, and *Tahú ná änä' nia' huna*.

I

Eyehé The young birds,
Eyehé The young birds.
Hé eé a ehé yuhé yu!
Hé eé a ehé yuhé yu!
The young Thunderbirds,
The young Thunderbirds.

II

Ninaa' niahu' na
Ninaa' niahu' na
Bi' taa' wu ha' nai sai
Bi' taa' wu ha' nai sai
Hi' naa' thi na' niwu' huna
Hi' naa' thi na' ni wu' huna.

I circle around
I circle around
The boundaries of the earth
The boundaries of the earth
Wearing the long wing feathers as I fly,
Wearing the long wing feathers as I fly.

The third song is sung to a quick joyful rhythm, and is unusual because only a part instead of all of the line is repeated.

III

Tahu' na' ana nia' huna

Na nisa' na, na nisa' na,
na nani' n ta' hu' na' ana' nia' huna,
   Tahu' na' ana' nia' huna
Na nisa' na, na nisa' na,
Na nani' na, ta' heti' nia huna,
   Ta' heti nia' huna.

My children, my children,
It is I who make the thunder as I circle about —
   The thunder as I circle about.
My children, my children
It is I who make the loud thunder as I circle about —
   The loud thunder as I circle about.

Another song in the ghost dance comes from the northern Arapaho.

     Nänisa' Tăqu' Chĭnachi' chibä iha'

    The seven venerable priests,
    The seven venerable priests,
    We see them
    We see them
    They all wear it on their heads
    They all wear it on their heads
    The Thunderbird
    The Thunderbird.
    Then I wept,
    Then I wept.

In his vision the singer sees a large camp of Arapaho, and seven priests of the Chi nachichi bat, sitting in the middle of the camp circle, each wearing on his head the Thunderbird headdress, as it used to be in the old days. This vision of the old life of his tribe makes him weep.

36

Among the Arapaho, the Crow is the sacred bird of the Ghost
Dance, revered as the messenger from the spirit world. The Crow
is depicted on the shirts, leggings and moccasins of the dancers, and
its feathers are worn on their heads, and there are many songs about
him during their version of the dance.

I

The crow is making a road,
He is making a road;
He has finished it,
He has finished it.
His children,
His children —

Then he collected them,
Then he collected them.
(i.e. on the farther side,
   the spirit side.)

II

The crow has called me,
The crow has called me
When the crow came for me,
When the crow came for me,
I heard him,
I heard him.

III

The crow is circling above me,
The crow is circling above me,
The crow having come for me,
The crow having come for me.

37

The singer in his trance vision saw circling above his head a crow, the messenger from the spirit world, to take him to his friends on the other side.

The Indians in the Owens Valley call the crow "Little Black Eagle." To them the eagle, the magpie, and the sage hen were the sacred birds in the Ghost Dance. The eagle for obvious reasons, the magpie because it is held sacred among the Piautes. The magpie of the Sierra Nevada is about the size of a crow, jet black except for its breast which is white, with a white spot on each wing. It has two long tail feathers with beautiful changeable luster. These were as highly prized among the Paiutes as eagle feathers by other tribes. It is a friendly bird, and used to visit the Paiute wickiups in small flocks. There are songs about it in their version of the Ghost Dance.

My children, my children,
I have given you magpie feathers again to wear on your heads
He i ye!

The sage hen belongs to the creation story of the Paiutes. At first the world was all water. Then the water began to go down and at last Kurangwa (Mount Grant) emerged from the water, near the south west end of Walker Lake. There was fire on its top (it may have been a volcano), and when the wind blew hard the water dashed over the fire and would have put it out, but the sage hen — hutsi — nestled down over it and fanned away the water with her wings. The heat scorched the feathers on the breast of the sage hen and they are black to this day. Afterward the Paiutes got their first fire from the mountain with the help of the rabbit, a great wonder-worker. As the water subsided other mountains appeared, until at last the earth was as it is now.

Other birds and animals are the central figures in the creation stories of many tribes. With the Paiutes it is the sage hen. But the Eagle takes precedence in all of them.

Sometimes, above the sweat lodges or the ceremony houses, eagles can be seen, circling with an escort of crows, or other birds,

39

The sage hen belongs to the creation story of the Paiutes.

even seagulls, and white birds from the north, like the snow goose. Sometimes there will be three of them without an escort. Sometimes one alone. They appear in the sky where there is nothing to be seen, an eyeblink before, and disappear in the same way, into nothingness. Some people do not see them. I have been in groups where two or three saw and watched intently, the Medicine Man among them, but most of those looking upward saw only the blue sky. Those who did see were not always those with the best physical eyesight, or the field glasses. I have been in encampments where the arrival of a bird behaving in an unnatural manner has caused some families to strike camp and move away, or conversely, once, to stay a night longer than they intended. In the morning friends arrived who would have had no hope of overtaking them if they had left the day before as originally planned. These things, no matter how often they occur, are usually set down to coincidence. But those who still pay attention to them, and to a number of other old "superstitions," often seem to come out ahead.

At first the world was all water.

VIII

THE EAGLE honored in all ages as the messenger of heaven is also, and not by accident, the emblem of the United States, a bridge between two opposing civilizations, Amerindian and white, and one of the few concepts common to both.

In India he was the Vahana which transported Vishnu and other Sun Gods, like the Babylonian Etana, whom he carried up to heaven. In Egypt the letter A was represented by an eagle, signifying the beginning, the day, the warmth of life. In Vedic tradition he was the messenger bearing the sacred soma, the ambrosia of the gods, from Indra, the Sky-God. In Greek mythology, he slept on the sceptre of Zeus and carried his thunderbolt. In Sarmation art he also carries the thunderbolt and is the emblem of battle, like the Amerindian Thunderbird of whom it is said: "The winged creature which crowns the totem pole is the Thunder Bird and represents the Great Creator or the great Creative Forces."

The eagle is the equivalent in the air of the lion on earth and is sometimes shown with a lion's head. In alchemy an eagle devouring a lion is the symbol of volatilization, his wings equal the spirit, his flight stands for imagination and spiritual victory. In ancient Persia he was Siena, "the ever blessed, glorious and mighty bird whose wings dim the very heavens."

In ancient Syria the eagle with human arms stood for sun-worship. He also conducted souls to immortality and in general was a messenger, a go-between the earth and unseen worlds. The Christians regarded him as a messenger from heaven, Theodoret compares the eagle to the spirit of prophecy, and St. Jerome said the eagle is the symbol of the Ascension and of prayer. In several mythologies the eagle's flight, because of its height and its swiftness stands for prayer rising to the Creator and grace descending to mortals.

43

The Eagle, catlinite pipehead by
Raymond Stone. The bowl is shown in the Eagle's
back, the stem fits into his tail.

Freemasons will remember the varied symbolism of the eagle in their higher degrees, and in the Bible there is constant mention of him:

"They that wait upon the Lord shall renew their strength; they shall mount up with wings as eagles."

"The bird of the air shall carry the voice and that which hath wings shall tell the matter."

Dante calls the eagle "the bird of God" and in cantos xix and xx of the Paradiso the eagle explains Divine Justice to the poet.

In Christian churches he is found bearing the weight of great bronze lecterns with the open book upon them, signifying that the eagle carries the Logos, the Word of Life to earth. There are also many images of the two-headed eagle, and of the eagle with a victim in his claws. The first is related to the Janus symbol and is usually shown in two colors of mystical importance, red and white. The second denotes the sacrifice of lower forces and instincts to higher spiritual principles.

His feathers were used by priests and medicine men for ceremonial and individual healing. The Egyptian Pharaohs wore a sacred cloak made of eagle feathers and such cloaks were also used by Amerindians. Eagle feathers were and still are sacred emblems and those who can earn the right to wear one are justly proud.

We find the image of his outspread wings here and there at Coso, and in the Owens Valley, more frequently in Nevada, and northward in Arapaho country almost everywhere. He is woven into baskets and blankets and beaded medallions and painted from coast to coast.

In the old days, only a Medicine Man who knew the sacred formula would dare to kill an eagle. Great misfortune would come upon anyone else who committed such a sacrilege. The Eagle Killer took with him a robe or some other valuable offering, and after shooting the eagle, making the proper prayers, and pulling out the tail and wing feathers, he covered the body with the robe and left it there as a peace offering to the spirit of the bird.

The procedure varied from tribe to tribe. Some took the body

The day on which one sees an eagle circling in the sky is a good luck day.

back to the lodge, and set it up on a pole laid across two forked sticks, driven into the ground. Then after prayers and purifications the feathers were stripped from the body as it hung.

Among the Caddo, Cherokee and other forest tribes, eagles were shot with bow and arrow or with a gun, but always according to ritual ceremonies. Among the prairie tribes of the plains they were never shot but must be captured alive in pitfalls and then strangled or crushed to death without the shedding of blood.

Whatever the method of death it was not to be undertaken lightly, for gain or for greed or for sport.

The day on which one sees an eagle circling in the sky is a good-luck day, with some exceptional messages or blessing from the "Great Mysterious," for now as in earlier civilizations, the Eagle is the Messenger, and not only symbolically. I have attended ceremonies where, when darkness was complete and after the first round of drumming and chanting stopped, we could hear the sweep of great wings, far above, too high to be reached from the ground, or in any way controlled or manipulated by the Medicine Man, lying bound and helpless shrouded in a blanket, or the people, sitting "in a sacred manner," motionless, crowded close together, so that if anyone attempted to move or to rise, all would have been aware of it.

Some have felt the grip of strong talons on their arms or hands, wings beat about their heads, their cheeks were framed in living feathers. There is also a high piping call, impossible to confuse with its physical counterpart, the eagle-bone whistle used in sacred dancing. It is not like that, nor any other sound that I have heard. I do not believe it could be produced and projected to circle above us by the Medicine Man, from his central position face downward on the ground. People who have never heard it suggest that this and other manifestations are caused by mass hypnotism. Perhaps, but I do not think so.

As the chanting and the drumming resume we can no longer hear the high piping call, but we can still feel rushing air displaced in a steady rhythm. When this pulsation ceases, something leaves the circle. Then, the Paiutes say, Grandfather Eagle, after he has looked the people over and given them his blessing, goes back to where he came from.

At the other end of the scale, the Humming Bird is also a Grandfather, in the Owens Valley. He too is a messenger, a healer, who sews up wounds with his needle-beak, and pierces to the heart of problems. Between him and the Eagle come a hierarchy of other birds, crows, hawks, owls, geese, seagulls, snowbirds, some of them Grandfathers in their own right to other tribes, in different parts of the country. Here they act as escorts and aides to the Eagle, and like the smaller birds and flying insects, they are "relatives" to the people.

The right procedure when a relative arrives with a message, is to greet him with welcoming words, (if we are not surrounded by the curious, before whom words would be indiscreet and might even throw doubts upon our sanity, or sobriety). When words are impossible, we must send out strong thoughts of welcome, and always we must try to understand what the message is. This may not be easy, but a grateful attitude, a sharpened intuition, an awareness of the interdependence of created things, and a knowledge of the messenger's characteristics, which we should also be developing in ourselves — these are helpful, and if we really want to become "catchers" and grasp communications sent to us, "the spirits" will help to make them plain.

PART TWO

IX

THE WHITE WORLD is apt to think that every Indian dance is a "war dance" and most whites refer to the Pipe as a "peace pipe," but these are only facets of Dance and Pipe. The Indians danced on many occasions and for many reasons. They do so still. There is the Cry Dance, the Ghost Dance, the Sun Dance, the Eagle Dance, the Buffalo Dance, the Deer Dance, the Snake Dance, the Corn Dance, etc., and only sometimes nowadays, as at Wounded Knee in 1973, the War Dance. There is also secular dancing at Pow Wows and demonstrations arranged for tourists.

When the white soldiers heard drumming and caught glimpses of bronzed men dancing, they were usually right in assuming that what they saw was a war dance. Most of the dancing at that time was in supplication to the Grandfathers for help against the savage invasion of the Indians' homeland.

When the white generals and leaders were invited to smoke the Pipe at the signing of treaties which later they intended to break, they were indeed seeing the Pipe smoked for the sealing of a peace. Therefore in the white man's mind there was a "war dance" and there was a "peace pipe," quaint customs which could be turned to advantage in fooling the Indians and keeping them quiet.

When they heard drumming, which might be for a hundred reasons, the invaders were convinced that "the savages" were getting ready to attack the settlements, and massacre the settlers, who had "conquered the wilderness and were opening up the New World." But the Indian, naturally, thought that the invaders were the savages, and he and his people the defenders of their own sacred land.

It puzzled him to hear of a "new world." His traditions taught him what recent excavations are beginning to show, and archeologists now report, that man existed (if man's existence is the criterion for "old" and "new") in ancient great civilizations on this conti-

51

nent long before recorded history. In fact the miscalled "Americas," which the miscalled "Indians" know as Turtle Island, may turn out to be the oldest part of the world inhabited by man.

In the same way the Indian knew nothing of a wilderness to be conquered. What the invaders called "wilderness" the Indian called "home," the familiar loved environment he shared with winged, four-footed, creeping brothers. The Great Spirit placed them where they should be and gave them the things that they would need, earth, water, air, fire, trees, vegetation, to be used, enjoyed and shared.

"When you don't use something the Grandfathers put out to be used, it will be taken from you, it will go away. Many things are not here now," an elder said to me.

The Indian ecology is based on the belief that everything created by the Great Holy is equally important and has its rightful place; that there is an interdependence of created things; that animals and plants are also people, whose welfare must be respected, who have a voice in the affairs of the world, a voice heard by the Grandfathers, and therefore animals and plants are "represented" in the Dances.

As for "conquering" our Mother Earth with bulldozers, explosions, strip-mining and every sort of pollution, this is desecration which will bring disaster upon all of us.

"Walk gently," the same old teacher told me, "listen to the breathing underneath the feet."

He also taught me the "Go slow way," the "No feel way," — have no resentment, no reaction to what others do or say. But he was having a slight feel-way, and smiling at himself for having it, when he told me "never say 'peace pipe.' That is whiteman talk."

Many books and papers have been written about the Pipe without revealing more than abc. The Pipe is Wakan, very holy magic. 'Magic' is not the right word, but one is drawn to use it to describe the experience of power in a working Pipe.

I knew a little about the Pipe, but nothing about dancing, when I went to my first Cry Dance in 1964. I had no idea what to expect.

I knew that it was a funeral service for a much respected man, that it would be held at a place north of Mammoth, that it would be acceptable for me and two friends who were staying with me, to attend, if we went with the Presbyterian Minister to one of the reservation missions who was to conduct the Christian service the day after the Cry Dance. This man and his family were known and trusted by his congregation and others in the valley.

So on a cold and windy November night beneath a climbing moon, I stood beside my friends, a composer and a sculptor, in a group of onlookers, on a slope overlooking a cleared space, with a big fire burning in the center of it. On one side there was the typical government-built box house where the family lived, beyond that the outhouse, and some indistinct sheds with shapes of cars and tractors round them.

The minister and his daughter went into the house to greet the bereaved family. Afterwards we saw them enter the circle standing round the fire, near a row of men in blankets and overcoats. These were the Cry-Dance Singers.

Presently the singing began, the dancers in the circle moved forward slowly, one behind the other, their left sides to the fire, holding something in their hands. Now and then they raised it above their heads, now and then they lowered it to their knees, in response to changes in the singing, but mostly they held it in front of them, fingers upward, elbows to their sides. It was too dark to see exactly what it was, even in the glow from the fire, but it seemed to be different colored strips of cloth.

The chief singer shouted "Heu!", the singing and the dancing ceased. The dancers turned toward the fire to warm themselves. A few slipped aside and went into the house. Others took their places. The Singer said "He ya!" Everything resumed. The song was different but the dance steps seemed to be the same stately step forward, half step back, balance and on.

There was another pause. A group came out of the house, two men supporting a woman between them. They moved slowly past the singers and the dancers, past the great fire, while everyone stood

still and silent. Presently they reached what I had not noticed before, the coffin on its high bier in the darkness, built so that it faced the firelit circle. Here they stopped. The woman stepped forward alone. Then the silence about us, the silence of the night itself, was filled with her "Cry," the sad, terrible sound of human grief, a lonely, proud, noble, almost cosmic lamentation. It pierced the darkness, it went travelling toward the mountains, it was everywhere.

After a moment others joined in, the singers chanted softly, accompanying her lament. This was her tribute to her dead husband, this was his family's and his tribe's farewell. When it ceased there was another long silence, through which she was led gently back, between the supporting men, into the house.

The dancing resumed. It would continue till the dawn. The sculptor went back to the car to sleep. The composer and I stood beneath our tree. We could neither of us have moved, we were rooted there, one with what we saw and heard, our bodies moving with the moving feet, our minds chanting the subtle ever-changing rhythms.

When the first light began to show over the Sierra, the dancers turned inward toward the fire, lifted what they were holding high, higher, balanced it, and flung it on the flames. Everything came to a stop, chanting, drums and dancing ceased. The circle broke and all went to the house.

Presently a man came out and walked towards us.

"Come in, come in," he said, "eating now. Coffee."

We followed him gladly, aware that we were frozen and exhausted.

The kitchen was small, the rooms behind it smaller, yet the whole throng was seated there, in silence, in rows along the walls, on the floor, and on the floors we could see through open doorways. Place was made for us beneath a window. Paper plates of food and cups of coffee were being handed round.

The Chief Singer, an old man, whom I came to know later, and who was held in great respect, said a long "grace" in Paiute. Eating

55

When the first light began to show
over the Sierra.

and low-voiced talk began. No one spoke to us. There were some curious stares, but no hostility, and here and there a tentative smile. The minister and his daughter had disappeared into an inner room with the widow and the immediate family. We were on our own, there and not there, among the group, of it and not of it.

Presently people began to leave. We rose too, looking about us for the man who had invited us to eat. We found him at the door.

"Goodba," he said, shaking our hands.

"Thank you for letting us be here."

"We appreciate."

He turned to the next in line. As we stepped outside the sun rose in full glow, sending rainbow prisms across the snow. We trudged to the car, hand in hand, woke the sculptor and started to drive home.

The sculptor babbled of shapes and effects of firelight, the composer and I were silent. Suddenly he burst out

"Why didn't I have my tape-recorder!"

"Oh come now," I said, "you wouldn't bring out a tape-recorder at a friend's funeral."

"I would if they buried him with sounds like that . . . ," he began to babble like the sculptor.

"Listen . . . ," and I told them what a Paiute taught me about tape recorders. "A song is made to be born, and heard by those who are meant to hear, and then it dies on the air. It is not to be put in a tin can and sold for money."

"But suppose no one is there to hear?"

"The Grandfathers hear it. It is sung for Them in the first place."

The composer shook his head. "Terrible! What a waste!"

"Non-Indians have only themselves to thank that Indians feel that way."

"I know, I know . . . but those rhythms and the undertones, the shifting stress . . . ."

Later the Indians took to using tape recorders themselves, to record their songs, and even allowed some of them to be taped, so long as they were not to be used commercially, but this decision was still ahead of them in 1964.

56

Presently the composer said: "I shall never forget . . . but I can't remember either . . . ."

I knew what he meant. In the Sweat Lodges and Ceremonies I know and understand the words that I sing. When I step outside I cannot reproduce them or remember what they mean.

We talked of the Cry, and the comfort it must be to express grief with such love, such truth and such finality.

The next time that I went to a Cry-Dance I was drawn into the circle to dance with the family and friends of the dead woman. I had met her several times, and also I was beginning to be accepted by the Paiute community.

I danced all night. The step came easily "back" to me. This was something I had always known. I had no separate existence. I was one with the dancers, one with the earth we trod, one with all creatures, those still here, those who had shed their overcoats and were gone ahead.

The cloth that I held, and raised and lowered with the other dancers, was part of the woman's clothing, torn into strips so that it could be distributed among many, and disposed of to the fire at the end of the dance.

When I stooped to pick it up and take my place in the circle, I saw that it was part of a dress. Did she wear it on a happy or a sad occasion? Was it a familiar friendly dress worn about the house, for sweeping or for baking bread? Holding it made me feel near to her.

When at the end I turned with the others and flung it on the fire, I understood that with it would go the unhappiness, faults, failings, bad luck, bitterness, pain, not only of this woman, but of her family, her tribe, her country and the world. It is a way of cleansing the human race of some of its heavy burdens. The departing give us this last gift. As they shared what they had when they were living here, now they share the purifying fire, setting us more free to continue our journey on the earth, as we help to set them free to travel the Milky Way, the Road of the Dead, to the Spirit world of the Grandfathers.

Gradually as I danced in the Cry Dances, I learned more about the Paiute burial way. It is a good one, comforting to the bereaved, and to the friends of the departed, who take actual psychic and physical part in the departure. Also it serves to draw the people more together. I felt closer to my Indian brothers and sisters after each dancing. I learned, too, that though the singing and the dance steps are the same, the experience in the circle varies with the lives and characters of the people being buried. Very different from the gentle serene vibrations I absorbed as I danced for an older woman, who had led a good life, a source of wisdom and strength to her people, and those which swept through me when I danced for a man who was an alcoholic, and who died badly, and the heavy horror-filled atmosphere round the death of a woman who was found in a ditch, apparently murdered. The Cry Dance is a deep experience for those who dance and those who sing.

The Singers are usually older, much respected men, who remember the old ways and "have" their songs, handed down to them from earlier Singers, or recaptured from the Spirit World in vision trance, from those who sang them while they were still on earth, taking them with them when they died.

Some of the Paiute Cry Dance Singers are training their sons and grandsons and other young men who are able and willing to undergo the training, to whom they will give their songs before they depart upon the Milky Way.

It is a proud thing to be a Singer. There are sacrifices to be made, a way of life to follow. No drinking and no drugs are two of the obvious requirements. Changes of mind and spirit are more subtle and more important.

X

I HAVE NO FIRST HAND knowledge or experience of the Dance most associated with the Paiutes, the Ghost Dance. I doubt if any white has. Even the descendants of Wovoka, the Prophet Medicine Man whose vision started it, go beneath the blanket completely whenever it is mentioned. They have never heard of Wovoka. There is no such thing as a Ghost Dance. If the questioner persists, the confrontation becomes a psychic blow to the solar plexus, strong enough to send you reeling back, or even, you feel, in another moment to knock you down, so far are your friends now turned against you. It is better to cease and desist, to accept the coffee or the tea, which you carefully refrain from calling "Squaw tea," and settle down to talk of other things.

Yet I do believe that the Ghost Dance is still danced in Nevada and parts of California on certain occasions. My conviction is supported by allusions, complicit glances, careful sudden silences, after the absence of a group of the most active people in the community, who have gone together somewhere important, fulfilling some important mission known to all but whites.

I also noticed that if I met them singly one by one as they returned, before they had time to agree upon a story, I was apt to hear many different reasons for the absence, many different versions which placed them in a number of unlikely locations separately, whereas I knew, and could gather from later references, that they were never apart. I had also a notion of at least the direction in which they went, and roughly the part of the country where they stayed, and I believe danced the Ghost Dance. But my beliefs have no validity, and there is no evidence to confirm them.

The Paiutes' attitude is not surprising. The failure of the Sioux rising, based on a misinterpretation of the Ghost Dance and Wovoka's teachings, culminated in the bloody massacre at Wounded Knee in 1890. After that there were bloody and savage reprisals on the part of the whites against everyone suspected of taking part in the Dancing. Bitter times increased for the Paiutes of Nevada and California. They remember them.

But the memory of Wounded Knee and the sufferings to follow is not the only reason for maintaining a strict silence with the whites. The essence of the Ghost Dance teaching, as Wovoka gave it to the world, is that "the time will come when the whole Indian race, living and dead, will be reunited upon a regenerated earth, to live a life of happiness, forever free from death, disease and misery. The white race will have no part in this, and will be left behind with the other things of earth that have served their temporary purpose, or else will cease entirely to exist. Meanwhile the people must dance the sacred dance, must do no harm to anyone, do right always, work well with the whites, and get along with them until the Day arrives. All things will be taken care of by the Great Spirit. Above all you must not fight, there must be no war." James Mooney heard this directly from Wovoka in 1892.

Other versions of the early doctrine come from various sources. In 1890 Captain J. M. Lee was told by "Captain Dick," a Paiute, who had it directly from "Sam," who had it from Wovoka:

" 'All Indians must dance, everywhere, keep on dancing. Pretty soon in next spring Big Man (Great Spirit) come. He bring back all game of every kind. The game be thick everywhere. All dead Indians come back and live again. They all young and have fine time. When Old Man comes this way, then all the Indians go to mountains, high up away from whites. Whites can't hurt Indians then. Then while Indians way up high, big flood comes like water and all white people die, get drowned. After that water go away and then nobody but Indians everywhere and game all kinds thick. Then medicine man tell Indians to send word to all Indians to keep up dancing and the good time will come. Indians who don't dance, who don't believe in this word, will grow little, just about a foot high, and stay that way. Some of them will be turned into wood and be burned in fire.' That's the way Sam tell me the medicine-man talk."

James Mooney reported that Lieutenant N. P. Phister, "who gathered a part of the material embodied in Captain Lee's report, confirms this general statement and gives a few additional particulars. "The flood is to consist of mingled mud and water, and when the faithful go up into the mountains, the skeptics will be left behind and will be turned to stone. The Prophet claims to receive these revelations directly from the Great Holy and the spirits of the dead Indians during his trances."

Other early versions of the Ghost Dance doctrine come from members of tribes like the Cheyenne, whose Medicine Man Porcupine visited Wovoka and received the teachings direct from him.

"My Father told me the earth was getting old and worn out and the people getting bad and that I was sent to renew everything as it used to be and make it better. He also told us that our dead were to be resurrected; that they would all come back to the earth and that the earth would be made big enough to contain us all; that we must tell all the people we met about these things. He spoke to us about fighting, and said that was bad and we must keep from it; that the earth was to be all good hereafter, and we must all be friends with one another. He told us that we were not to quarrel or fight or strike each other or shoot one another; that the whites and the Indians were to be all one people."

This is one of the few statements that the two races are to live together as one, and it is not considered as part of the essential doctrine. It is also sometimes interpreted "are to live as one until the day of the great change arrives."

Most tribes believed that, in the words of an Arapaho who spoke English: "This earth too old, grass too old, trees too old, our lives too old. Then all be new again." The plains tribes also believed that the rivers, the mountains and the earth were worn out and must be renewed, they also believed that both Indians and whites must die at the same time, to be resurrected in new but separate worlds.

The Walapai, in 1891, were expecting the Indian redeemer to appear on earth some time within three or four years. They were particularly anxious to have it understood that their "intentions

61

were not hostile towards the whites and that they desired to live in peace with them until the redeemer came, but that then they would be unable to prevent their destruction even if they wished."

James Mooney observed "The manner of the final change and the destruction of the whites has been variously interpreted as the doctrine was carried from its original center. East of the mountains it is commonly held that a deep sleep will come on the believers, during which the great catastrophe will be accomplished, and the faithful will awake to immortality on a new earth. The Shoshoni of Wyoming say this sleep will continue four days and nights and that on the morning of the fifth day all people will open their eyes in a new world where both races will dwell together forever. The Cheyenne, Arapaho, Kiowa, and others say that the new earth with all the resurrected dead from the beginning, and with the buffalo the elk, and other game upon it, will come from the west and slide over the surface of the present earth, as the right hand might slide over the left. As it approaches the Indians will be carried upward and alight on it by the aid of the sacred dance feathers which they wear in their hair and which will act as wings to bear them up. They will then become unconscious for four days, and on waking out of their trance will find themselves with their former friends in the midst of all the old time surroundings . . . ."

Sitting Bull, the Arapaho Medicine Man, thought that this new earth as it advances will be preceded by a wall of fire which will drive the whites across the water to their original and proper country, while the Indians will be enabled by means of the sacred feathers to surmount the flames and reach the promised land. When the expulsion of the whites has been accomplished the fire will be extinguished by a rain continuing twelve days.

Some Medicine Men of some tribes believed that the good and great and humble of any race would be saved, that in fact "the meek will inherit the earth." All the tribes except the Sioux believed that the destruction or removal of the whites was to be accomplished entirely by supernatural means, by the Great Spirit, but the Sioux, carrying what they understood of the doctrine a logical

62

— to their minds — step further, decided that if the millenium was to be preceded by the annihilation of the whites, they would hasten the great day by rising and fighting a holy war. They did, and were defeated and went down to disaster, thus postponing indefinitely, but not forever, the salvation promised by Wovoka, who, it was remembered too late, had also said "Do no harm to anyone," "Do right always," "You must not fight," "live in peace with all men, and with the whites," while waiting for the Great Spirit to take care of all men when the time is right.

At the time of the earthquake near Los Angeles in 1971, my Indian friends seemed concerned. One of them said to me, "If all the birds leave the sky, if you don't see any bird for three days, then you must leave too."

"Where shall I go?"

He pointed vaguely to the mountains.

"The Grandfathers will tell you."

Others came to see me, and went out of their way to be affectionately kind. Their attitude reminds me of my sister's Spanish servants in Majorca, who believing we were damned, being protestants, and yet being fond of us, wanted to be sure we had all the little joys and comforts they could give us in this world, since those were all we could have, since we had nothing good or happy to look forward to.

In the same way I believe my Indian friends are sorry for individual whites whom they know and like. Perhaps a corner may be found for us. Perhaps — more likely — our own grandfathers will take us somewhere else.

Meanwhile they spoil us, with love and little presents, because we are their whiteys, and unfortunately doomed.

They tell us to smudge ourselves and our homes and our cars, and keep them well smudged always, with plenty of the sacred sage, "for protection," as the Israelites were told to distinguish their homes at the time of the Passover.

But not once, not one of my Indian friends has ever broken faith to tell me anything whatever of the Ghost Dance, or admit that such a dance exists, or that there ever was a prophet called Wovoka.

XI

Wovoka was born somewhere between 1856 and 1858, in Mason Valley in Nevada, near the sacred mountain of the Paiute, and not far from the sacred Pyramid Lake. He never left his native valley. Those who wished to hear his teachings had to come to him.

He was the son of Tavibo, also known as Waughzeewaughber, a "dreamer," a prophet, but not, according to Wovoka, a Medicine Man. Nor did he consider himself a Medicine Man, but also, a dreamer, a prophet, a leader of his people, and later at the height of his enormous influence not only over the Paiutes, but most of the western tribes, he allowed himself to be called the Messiah, and even Jesus, the Paiute Jesus Christ, come again to earth to save his people.

Wovoka or Wuvoka, meaning "cutter," from the root verb "to cut," was also known as Wevokar, Wopokahte, Kwohitsauk, Cowejo, Koit-tsow, Quoitze Ow, and he had English names as well, Jack Wilson, Jackson Wilson, Jack Winson, John Johnson. He acquired his English name from the Wilson family for whom he worked as a boy, after his father's death, when he was about fourteen, and later, on and off, especially when he was married, and needed to support his family.

The Paiutes of that part of Nevada were not as brutally suppressed and persecuted as they were elsewhere because the first ranchers needed their help, and took them under their protection, looking upon them more or less as peons. The Paiutes have always been excellent workers, noted for their horsemanship, and their expert handling of the "white man's buffalo," his cattle, and other ranch work.

Today in Nevada, and in the nearby Owens Valley, the Paiutes breed and raise horses, and work with them, though like most Indians they are not interested in cattle. Cows are rare on reservations.

64

Cow's milk is not a valued part of Indian food. Beef is not as good as venison, and far inferior to buffalo.

Wovoka learned the white ways and adopted some of them. He wore white clothing, but he lived in a traditional Paiute wickiup and there he and his family lived in the Paiute way. The Wilsons were understanding. They were more than mere employers to Wovoka, they became his lifelong friends. The Wilson sons remained friendly, even after he had left the ranch and begun his work as prophet and messiah. It may have been with them in mind that he so often and so firmly stressed that there was to be no war against the whites, no hatred of the whites, that on the contrary it was the Great Spirit's will that his children should work well and in harmony with all men until the day when "snowy earth comes gliding" and all things are renewed.

He was certainly influenced by this white family for whom he worked, and with whom he lived for many years until he married and set up his wickiup. The Wilsons taught him English, they taught him to read, and — not so well — to write. They introduced him to the Bible, and gave him his ideas of Jesus, whom later he believed himself to be.

His personal contacts with the whites were not as sad, as bitter, as shocking as those he came to hear about among other tribes. When he learned what was happening to Indians all over "Turtle Island" he was shocked, grieved, and for a time made physically, seriously ill, but still he never wavered from the teaching given to him in trance:

"There must be no war. Fighting, killing is forbidden. Do no harm to anyone. Do right always."

Early in his teaching he condemned the cruel burial rites common among all tribes. "When your friends die, you must not kill your horses, must not gash your bodies with knives, nor let your wives cut off their hair and be made to bleed. When your friends die, you must not cry, because you will all be united again." Instead of these old customs there would be the Cry-Dance as the Paiutes practice it today.

His teachings came to him in vision-trances, of which he had many. The most important of these long cataleptic-seeming seizures, coincided with a total eclipse of the sun, on January 1st 1889. The Paiutes were awed and frightened by this "death of the sun," which they observed with drumming, singing and cries against the enemy devouring it. The going away of their prophet at such a time impressed them greatly and added to his growing authority among them.

He lay for four days and four nights, seemingly dead. When he returned to consciousness on the morning of the fifth day, he told his wife and those who had watched by his body, that he had seen the Great Holy and all the people who were dead, in another world, that Numin'a had told him to go back to his people and teach them a new dance, that if they danced it well and faithfully they would be able to go to the other world as he did and see their dead ones too.

"This dance that we teach you," the Grandfathers told him, "has never been danced before. It is the Spirit Dance of the Other world."

The people must dance it for four nights and the morning of the fifth day. It must be danced in a circle facing inwards, with men and women dancers, hand in hand, first a man, then a woman, then a man. The faces of the dancers must be marked with sacred paint from ochre-colored rocks in the valley. This is the same "paint" the Paiutes still take from Coso and other places for healing and ceremonial purposes.

The dancers must dance faithfully and often, at least once every six weeks. They must not hurt anyone, they must not fight, they must not drink whiskey, they must not refuse to work for the white people, they must no longer hate the whites. Always they must do right.

These teachings, Wovoka said, were "alla same Jesus," and he, Wovoka, was "alla same Jesus."

He would dance in the circle with his people, as Jesus danced with his disciples. It is interesting that the Gnostic traditions, in

Fragments of a Faith Forgotten, refer to a special dance which Jesus danced in a circle with his disciples. Wovoka also said "there was a king who danced in the Bible, David was his name."

There were songs to go with the dancing, Wovoka said, sacred songs which he would teach his people, and they must sing them when they danced.

> Fog! Fog!
> Lightning! Lightning!
> Whirlwind! Whirlwind!
>
> There is dust from the whirlwind,
> There is dust from the whirlwind,
> There is dust from the whirlwind.
> The whirlwind on the mountain,
> The whirlwind on the mountain,
> The whirlwind on the mountain.
> The rocks are ringing,
> The rocks are ringing,
> The rocks are ringing.
> They are ringing in the mountains,
> They are ringing in the mountains,
> They are ringing in the mountains.

Paiute singing is slow and stately, like the circling of an eagle. There is a plaintive depth in it not found in the songs of other tribes. It well suits the slow and solemn step of the Ghost Dance. The dancers move from right to left, clockwise, or rather sunwise, lifting the left foot hardly off the ground, moving it slightly to the left, bringing the right foot exactly into the place the left foot has just abandoned. The Shoshoni call it the "dragging dance."

It is a different step from other Indian dances, and the dancers stand differently. They stand in a circle, facing inwards and hold one another's hands. The Cry Dance is also a circle, but no one touches another, and the dancers follow each others' backs, also they move counter sun-wise.

I have seen Indian dancing in Arizona and Wyoming which seems to be in free patterns, each dancer travelling his own circle and doing his own version of the steps, with no regard for what another dancer may be doing, as they weave in and out of the crowded dance space, attending strictly to their own ritual unfolding of the pattern forms. As embassies from different tribes came to Wovoka to be instructed in the Ghost Dance, they took the steps back to their people, and these were always danced in the same way, with the circle arranged in the same way, but the singing and the words of the songs were Arapaho, or Kiowa, or Caddo or Sioux, and the stress was sometimes different, on the Eagle or the Crow or the Magpie, or the Buffalo or the sacred Shirt.

The purpose of the Dance remained the same, to send as many dancers as possible into a deep trance, so that they could join their dead relatives and friends, and bring back confirmation of Wovoka's teachings about the land of the spirits, and by faithfully dancing, bring about the coming of this kind of a "new world."

The Arapaho songs stressed the Crow.

> Stand ready,
> Stand ready.
> So that when the Crow calls you,
> So that when the Crow calls you
> You will see him,
> You will see him.
>
> The Crow has given me the signal,
> The Crow has given me the signal.
> When the Crow makes me dance,
> When the Crow makes me dance,
> He tells me when to stop,
> He tells me when to stop.

This was the closing song of the dance, but later another closing song took its place:

This says our father, the Crow,
This says our father, the Crow
Go around five times more -
Go around five times more -
Says the father,
Says the father.

There are other references to the Crow:

The Crow is running,
The Crow is running,
He will hear me,
He will hear me.

meaning that the Grandfather will hear the prayer the dancer is offering, and be quick to answer it.

There is also an interesting reference to the magpie:

My children, my children,
I have given you magpie feathers to wear on your heads
Thus says our mother,
Thus says our mother.

It is interesting because it refers to the Giver, as "my mother," *nena*, instead of "our father," *hesuanin*, as in:

There is our father -
There is our father -
We are dancing as he wishes us to dance,
We are dancing as he wishes us to dance,
Because our father has given it to us,
Because our father has given it to us.

Perhaps the reference to "Mother" in the magpie song is in honor of the Sun, which in Arapaho is feminine, as the Moon is masculine.

When we dance until daylight, our father, the Moon,
Takes pity on us - ahe'e'ye'!
When we dance until daylight, our father, the Moon,
Takes pity on us - ahe'e'ye'!
The father says so - ahe'e'ye'!
The father says so - ahe'e'ye'!

There are songs to the Morning Star:

My children, my children,
It is I who wear the Morning Star on my head,
It is I who wear the Morning Star on my head;
I show it to my children,
I show it to my children,
Says the father,
Says the father.

Father, the Morning Star!
Father, the Morning Star!
Look on us, we have danced until daylight,
Look on us, we have danced until daylight.
Take pity on us - Hi'i'i'!
Take pity on us - Hi'i'i'!

The Kiowa Ghost Dance songs stress the coming of the father,
and of the spirit army, and the return to the old good ways in a
new world.

The father will descend,
The father will descend.
The earth will tremble,
The earth will tremble.
Everybody will arise,
Everybody will arise.
Stretch out your hands,
Stretch out your hands.

71

"Stretch out your hands" (upward in worship).
Carved figure by Raymond Stone.

The spirit army is approaching,
The spirit army is approaching,
The whole world is moving onward,
The whole world is moving onward.
See! Everybody is standing watching,
See! Everybody is standing watching.
Let us all pray,
Let us all pray.

In this song the Kiowa verb imza'nteahe' dal implies that the spirits are coming on like an army or a great herd of animals. The termination he'dal means that this is a matter of report or common belief, not of personal knowledge.

The father shows me the road,
The father shows me the road.
I went to see my friends,
I went to see my friends,
I went to see the dances,
I went to see the dances.

Whenever "the road" is mentioned it usually refers to the road of the dead, the Milky Way, and the dances here mean the dances of the dead relatives and friends in the Spirit Land.

I scream because I am a bird,
I scream because I am a bird,
I bellow like a buffalo,
I bellow like a buffalo.
The boy will rise up,
The boy will rise up.

This song was composed by Pa-guadal, "Red Buffalo," at a Ghost Dance held on Walnut Creek in the summer of 1893, under the direction of the prophet Pa-ingya. The purpose of the dance

Carved figure of Buffalo by Raymond Stone.

was to gain contact with Red Buffalo's son who had recently died. Red Buffalo apparently was a member of the Eagle Dance, and followed the Eagle Way — "I scream because I am a bird," but his father was a Buffalo Medicine Man, who had left his knowledge to his son. Therefore Red Buffalo, although he was an Eagle, could and did "bellow like a buffalo."

The white man reporting this incident, thought that the Indians were expecting an actual physical appearance of the dead boy, and he remarks "the boy was not resurrected." But, if there was dancing, it is probable that the dancers and the Indians watching them knew the meeting between father and son must take place in trance, in the Spirit World.

The Kiowa songs were pragmatic. They were concerned with the coming new day, and what it would bring to the people, and how best to comply with the necessary conditions which would bring it about.

> The spirit host is advancing, they say,
> The spirit host is advancing, they say.
> They are coming with the buffalo, they say,
> They are coming with the buffalo, they say.
> They are coming with the new earth, they say,
> They are coming with the new earth, they say.
>
> The spirit is approaching,
> The spirit is approaching.
> He is going to give me a bird tail,
> He is going to give me a bird tail.
> He will give it to me in the tops of the cottonwoods,
> He will give it to me in the tops of the cottonwoods.

The "bird tail" refers to the sacred feathers worn on the heads of the dancers, and held in their hands. The singer must climb high, that is have high aspirations, if he is to be able to receive it.

74

My father has much pity for us,
My father has much pity for us.
I hold out my hands toward him and cry,
I hold out my hands toward him and cry.
In my poverty I hold out my hands toward him and cry,
In my poverty I hold out my hands toward him and cry.

Because I am poor,
Because I am poor,
I pray for every living creature,
I pray for every living creature.

This song was usually followed by the Kiowa Cry Dance wail.
One of the best descriptions of the Kiowa hope for a return to the
old ways is found in the song "He makes me dance with arrows."

He makes me dance with arrows,
He makes me dance with arrows.
He calls the bow my father,
He calls the bow my father.
Grandmother, persevere,
Grandmother, persevere.

"He calls the bow my father," with all that it implies of trust and
reliance on the ancient ways is a touchingly beautiful line, and
"Grandmother, persevere," evokes the steady strength of the older
women, their vital help in maintaining the well-being of the tribe.
    The Kiowa have also given us a version of "God made man in his
own image."

My father had pity on me
My father has had pity on me,
I have eyes like my father's,
I have hands like my father's,
I have legs like my father's,
I have a form like my father's.

75

The Caddo Ghost Dance songs deal chiefly with the trance journey itself, the going up to the Spirit Land, the Eagle and the return of the Eagle feathers to be used in the dance.

> All our people are going up
> All our people are going up,
> Above to where the father dwells,
> Above to where the father dwells,
> Above to where our people live,
> Above to where our people live.
>
> All the people cried when I returned,
> All the people cried when I returned,
> Where the father dwells above,
> Where the father dwells above.

This is a trance-song brought back by a girl who visited the Spirit land and saw all her dead friends there. When she had to leave this land where the father dwells, her friends wept.

> Come on, Caddo, we are all going up,
> Come on, Caddo, we are all going up
> To the great village, He'e'ye'!
> To the great village, He'e'ye'!
> With our father above,
> With our father above where he dwells on high — He'e'ye'!
> Where our mother dwells — He'e'ye'!

This was sung near the beginning or the early middle of the dance to remind the people of the purpose of the dance. The village above is the spirit land, but more than that it is a great encampment, the Indian Celestial City, Jerusalem the Golden. Our mother is the earth, which also has its place in heaven.

76

The feather has come back from above — He'e'ye'!
The feather has come back from above — He'e'ye'!
Is he doing it? Is he doing it?
The feather has returned from on high — He'e'ye'!
The feather has returned from on high — He'e'ye'!
Is he doing it? Is he doing it?

The last Caddo Eagle-killer died sometime in the 1880's, and knowledge of the Eagle-killing ritual died with him. After that the Caddo people had to go without Eagle feathers, or trade with the Kiowa for them, or obtain them from other tribes. Then Sitting Bull came back from the Spirit land and gave the feathers to the leaders of the dance. This made it acceptable for man or woman of any tribe to get the feathers in any way they could, with due regard to the sacred nature of the bird, and to wear them when they were qualified to do so.

"Is he doing it? Is he doing it?" means "Is this the doing of the Father, or of Sitting Bull? Is he bringing back the feather?" and the answer "yes" is understood.

The eagle feather headdress from above,
The eagle feather headdress from above,
From the eagle above, from the eagle above;
It is that feather we wear,
It is that feather we wear.

This is a thanksgiving verse, in the dance, that the feather has returned, and can be used in the old ritual way.

There is an eagle above,
There is an eagle above;
All the people are using it,
All the people are using it.
See! They use it,
See! They use it.

77

This too is a reference to the proper use of the feather. "There is an eagle above" can be taken in two ways, as a reference to the eagle headdress worn by the dancers, or to the actual circling of an eagle above the dancers, as eagles sometimes circle above other ceremonies and are seen by the people taking part in them.

The Cheyenne, like the Arapaho, with whom they have always been closely related in friendship, are part of the Algonquin nation. They were great warriors, "distinguished for their desperate courage and pride of bearing," James Mooney writes of them, and Clark in his *Indian Sign Language* says "As a tribe they have been broken and scattered, but in their wild and savage way they fought well for their country, and their history during the past few years (before 1890) has been written in blood."

Their language is more sibilant and harsh than Arapaho, and they usually joined the Arapaho Ghost Dancing, and sang the Arapaho songs. But they did, and probably still do, have their own songs.

> Well, my children, well my children,
> When you meet your friends again,
> When you meet your friends again,
> The earth will tremble,
> The earth will tremble,
> The summer cloud
> Will give it to us
> Will give it to us.

"The earth will tremble" refers to the earthquake expected when the new world meets the old.

> Our father has come,
> Our father has come.
> The earth has come.
> The earth has come,

79

It is rising, it is rising,
It is humming, it is humming.

The new earth makes a humming or rolling sound as it comes swiftly. This is Porcupine's song, the Medicine Man of the northern Cheyenne (mentioned in Chapter X), who brought Wovoka's teachings directly back to them.

The Cheyenne's sacred bird in the Ghost Dance is the Crow.

My father, my father,
I come to him, I come to him,
The crow, the crow,
I cry like it, I cry like it,
CAW I say, CAW I say.

The crow, the crow,
He is circling around,
He is circling around,
His wing, his wing —
I am dancing with it.
I am dancing with it.
The crow, the crow,
I saw him when he flew down,
I saw him when he flew down,

To the earth, to the earth.
He has renewed our life,
He has renewed our life,
He has taken pity on us,
He has taken pity on us.

I am coming in sight — Ehe'ee'ye'!
I am coming in sight — Ehe'ee'ye'!
I bring the whirlwind with me — E'yahe'eye'!
I bring the whirlwind with me — E'yahe'eye'!
That you may see each other —
That you may see each other.

The whirlwind is mentioned in many ghost dance songs, among many different tribes. It has a special place in Paiute beliefs. Several Paiute friends have warned me not to look directly at the "little whirlwind," the dust-devil, that springs up in the desert. If I did not look, I would not attract him, and bring danger to me. The bigger whirlwind evidently precedes the coming of the new world and sweeps the way before it.

The Cheyenne believe that they came out of a river which they call the "River of the Turtles," which some think may be the headwaters of the Mississippi in Minnesota.

> My children, my children,
> Here is the river of turtles,
> Here is the river of turtles,
>
> Where the various living things,
> Where the various living things,
> Are painted their different colors,
> Are painted their different colors.
> Our father says so,
> Our father says so.
>
> I waded into the yellow river,
> I waded into the yellow river,
> This was the Turtle river into which I waded,
> This was the Turtle river into which I waded.

Rivers are important to the Cheyenne. They are mentioned in many songs. The Turtle is a sacred Grandfather to many tribes, and sweat lodges are built in the shape of a turtle.

> My father — E'yehe'! Ehe'eye'!
> My father — E'yehe'! E'he'eye'!
> When I first met him — Ehe'eye'!
> When I first met him — Ehe'eye'!
> "In the blue-green water — He'eye!

81

In the blue-green water — He'eye'!
You must take a bath — He'eye'!
You must take a bath" — He'eye'!
Thus he told me, thus he told me — He'!

The Arapaho, the Cheyenne and some other tribes have no separate word for blue and for green. The two colors apparently are the same to them. I know that once when I was told to bring a green cloth to an Arapaho ceremony, it was put among the blue "flags," and there were other green ones there.

The Sioux, who misinterpreted Wovoka's Ghost Dance doctrine of peace with all men, were smarting under particularly atrocious treatment by the whites. They grasped as desperate people will, at any hope of relief. The Paiutes did not use a Ghost shirt, a war-shirt, which would be bulletproof. This would have been completely contrary to the whole concept and spirit of the original Ghost Dance. Just where the Ghost shirt originated, is not clear. It may have started with some vague remembrance of the Mormon "endowment robe" worn by initiates, and considered to protect the wearer from all evil.

The Mormons took a particular interest in the Indians, whom they believed were Lamanites, and part of the Mormon people. Paiutes, Shoshonis, Bannocks and Utes had all been received into the Mormon church and given endowment robes. It may be from some of these Mormon converts that the idea of a special robe or shirt, decorated with symbols as the Mormon robe was, came into being. If it protected the wearer from evil, it would be bulletproof, and if it were bulletproof, those wearing it need have no fear of the whites. They could sweep them away, to prepare the coming of the new world, since it was only the white men's guns that won them battles against Indians.

From the wearing of a ghost shirt to the horrible disaster at Wounded Knee was only a short and fatal step. The Sioux took it, spurred on by their chiefs and by the Medicine Men and leaders in the dance, and brought disaster on the Indian peoples of all the tribes, postponing indefinitely, perhaps forever, the coming of the prophesied new world.

The Sioux sang several good dance songs:

> The whole world is coming,
> A nation is coming, a nation is coming,
> The Eagle has brought the message to the tribe,
> The father says so, the father says so,
> Over the whole earth they are coming,
> The buffalo are coming, the buffalo are coming,
> The crow has brought the message to the tribe,
> The father says so, the father says so.

The return of the dead and of the buffalo is announced by two sacred birds, the Eagle — in this case the war eagle (wanbali), from whose feathers war bonnets are made, and the Crow, thought of as usual as the messenger between the spirit world and the earth.

Many of the Sioux songs refer to the Shirt:

> It is I who make these sacred things,
> Says the father, says the father,
> It is I who make the sacred shirt,
> Says the father, says the father.
> It is I who make the pipe,
> Says the father, says the father.
>
> I have given you my strength
> Says the father, says the father,
> The shirt will cause you to live,
> Says the father, says the father.

Nothing is more tragic than accounts of the dying at Wounded Knee, taking off the shirts they thought had betrayed them. But Wovoka when he heard what had happened as the direct result of his teachings was appalled, and struck to the heart by what he con-

sidered was the Sioux's betrayal of him and of his peaceful teaching. "Harm no one. Kill no one. War is not the way. Be in peace with all men."

The Paiute Ghost Dance songs are slow, soft songs of the coming of a new world which will be like the coming of spring.

> The wind stirs the willows,
> The wind stirs the willows,
> The wind stirs the willows,
> The wind stirs the grasses,
> The wind stirs the grasses,
> The wind stirs the grasses.
>
> The cottonwoods are growing tall,
> The cottonwoods are growing tall,
> The cottonwoods are growing tall.
> They are growing tall and green,
> They are growing tall and green,
> They are growing tall and green.

In a world where so much is so badly and quickly misunderstood, it is better to sing songs which can be easily explained away, and it is also prudent to deny that there was ever a Paiute prophet named Wovoka, or a Ghost Dance which he gave to the world. Silence on such sacred matters may help to hasten the coming of the long-awaited whirlwind which shall usher in a new and better world.

Wovoka died in 1932. He is buried next to his wife, Mary, in the Indian cemetery on the Walker Lake Reservation, in Nevada.

"The cottonwoods are growing tall."

XII

THE SUN DANCE is a dance of renewal, first of the man or woman setting it in motion, then the family, the tribe, the nation, the country, the world. It is set in motion to fulfill a vow made by an individual, but it requires the widespread cooperation of groups within the tribe to bring it to its great conclusion. It lasts for eight days of special and exacting rituals.

It was most often danced among the tribes of the Great Plains, particularly the Iroquois, Arapaho, Cheyenne, Sioux and Dakota. There is an excellent account of the Dakota Sun Dance in *The World's Rim* by Hartley Burr Alexander, and of the Oglala Sioux Sun Dance in *The Sacred Pipe* by John Epes Brown. The Iroquois Sun Dance is well described in *Sweet Medecine*, by Peter J. Powell, but it is the Arapaho Sun Dance for which we have the most comprehensive, well documented, well photographed account by George A. Dorsey, in 1903, sponsored by the Field Columbian Museum, using material gathered in Western Oklahoma from two performances, in 1901, and 1902, which he attended, at a time when it was feared the celebration of the Sun Dance might die out altogether under the relentless persecution of the United States Indian Office, and its agents, ignorant of the true meaning of the ceremony, ignorant of almost everything to do with Indian philosophy and way of life.

"Dancing is diminishing, and the heathenish annual ceremony, termed the Sun Dance will, I trust, from the way it is losing ground be soon a thing of the past." V. T. Gillicuddy, Agent Pine Ridge, Annual Report, 1882.

"The barbarous festival known as the 'sun dance' has lost ground." James G. Wright, Agent Rosebud, Annual Report 1883.

"They have also made great progress in abandoning many of their old customs, noticeably that of the sun dance, which for the

87

Snakes are considered guardians of the springs of life.

first time in the history of the Oglala Sioux and Northern Cheyennes was not held. The abandonment of such a barbarous, demoralizing ceremony, antagonistic to civilization and progress...,"
etc., etc. V. T. McGillicuddy, Agent Pine Ridge, Annual Report
1884.

Fortunately, in spite of this barbarous and demoralizing attitude
on the part of the occupying authorities, the guardians of the sacred
dance were able to resist its complete extinction, to keep the spirit
of it alive in the hearts and minds of the people, and as soon as better
understanding and more generous times permitted, to revive it in
most of its ancient splendor. The performances described by Dorsey were handicapped by having to be given in the presence of
white observers, and by the loss of the traditional sacred objects
and regalia, the buckskins, belts, headdresses, eagle feathers, baskets,
drums, etc. confiscated, looted, burned in great bonfires, and otherwise destroyed as a matter of deliberate policy by the conquerors.
Hawkan, the Director, Chief Priest, Lodge Maker of these two
dances, prayed at the beginning of the great Eight Days:

"We are young in the ways of our forefathers, *and old things
have to a certain extent gone out of existence*, and we are under
obligations to call upon you for your sympathy." Then he asked
that the substitutes they were compelled to use, now that they had
nothing, might be acceptable, that the world and all the peoples in
it might continue to be blessed.

This is surely one of the most dignified understatements of what
had happened to the Indian people, unless the interpreter softened
the wording for the sake of the white men present.

The Sun Dance is not performed in the Owens Valley. It is not
a part of the Paiute culture, but Paiutes and Arapahos intervisit
and sometimes attend the same ceremonies. Also a knowledge of
the ritual unfolding of the Arapaho Sun Dance is very helpful in
deciphering the Rock Drawings, especially the wheels, circles,
discs, crosses and shields.

The Wheel, next to the sacred Pipe in the keeping of the Northern Arapaho, is the most revered object possessed by the tribe. It is

89

*Snakes are considered guardians of the springs of
life. Coso petroglyphs.*

an integral part of the Sun Dance ceremony, and also used in other ceremonies. The Keeper of the Wheel is an important Chief, entrusted with protecting the Wheel from desecration, harm or violence. When not in use, i.e. when somebody has not made a vow to "wrap the Wheel," or when it is not in the Sun Dance or other ceremonies, it hangs on a pole or tripod at the back of the Keeper's Lodge, wrapped in colored cloths and buckskin.

The Wheel itself, *Hehotti*, is about eighteen inches in diameter, made of wood, tapered at both ends to represent the head and tail of a snake, not a poisonous snake, this is the little harmless one found by the edge of ponds and streams. The snake is the universal symbol of primeval energy, of Force. In India, snakes are considered guardians of the springs of life and of immortality, also of hidden treasure, they are symbols of the wisdom of the deeps and of the Mysteries. The little snake of the Wheel wears blue beads around its neck, in the place of the red berries worn before the coming of the traders. The red stood for life. Now the blue beads of the necklace reflect the sky, and blue is also the color of friendship.

Four inside markings, *Hitanni*, refer to the Four Old Men, the Keepers of the four world quarters, the four elements of life, the four courses, the four divides, summer, winter, day and night. They also represent the Thunderbird.

Four complete sets of an eagle's tail feathers are attached to the Wheel by short buckskin thongs. An eagle tail has twelve feathers, so there should be forty-eight feathers round the rim, but when necessary these are reduced by half, a single tail feather is divided into four so that two eagle feathers provide six feathers each to the four marking places.

These feathers represent the Thunderbird. There is an Arapaho legend that once the Wheel escaped and flew away. It was seen flying over the people. Presently it landed in front of them and changed into an eagle. Then it flew away again, and after awhile, when it did not return, a replica of it had to be made, in a difficult and complicated ceremony, with the help of a strange young man, who may have been a supernatural being.

91

A wheel with a central hub. Coso petroglyphs.

The inside rim of the Wheel is painted red, the outer rim is black. Red symbolizes blood, life, the people; black, in the Arapaho system, stands for the earth. The Wheel represents Creation, as do the wheels and circles on the rocks, varying depictions of the Great Medicine Wheel of the Universe, where everything created has its appropriate place.

One form of the circle, appearing frequently among the rock drawings at Coso and in the Owens Valley, shows a wheel, with a central hub, and spikes or radii joining the hub to the circumference. On the last day of the Sun Dance, in earlier days, the dancers, attached to the central Altar Pole by taut thongs of leather or rawhide fastened through the flesh of their breasts, leaned backward, staring at the sun, representing in their persons the interdependence of the created, and their relationship with the Creator, in the great wheeling dance of the Universe, where all things move inward, from the circumference to the Center. The spoked wheel on the rocks may be a reminder of this part of the Sun Dance, and share the same symbolic meaning.

Everything about the Wheel is symbolic, and so is the pole or tripod on which it is suspended. The Wheel represents in its most elemental form a symbol of the creation of the world, with glyphs of the sun, earth, sky, water and the four winds, but there is a deeper meaning associated with ancient symbols of the Wheel, the Wheel of Life, Ezekial's Wheel, the Zodiac, etc., also the symbolism of the serpent swallowing its tail.

Jakob Boehme, 16th-century mystic, wrote in his confessions: "The Being of God is like a Wheel, wherein many wheels are made one in another, upwards, downwards, crossways, and yet continually turn all of them together. At which indeed, when a man beholds the wheel, he highly marvels."

As Krappe has pointed out, the concept of the sun as a wheel and of ornamental wheels as solar emblems, is widespread in ancient civilizations and among the Aryans and Semites. If the sun is the source of light and of spiritual illumination, it is easier to understand the Buddhist doctrine of the Wheel, as a symbolic synthesis of

93

The spoked wheel on the rocks. Coso petroglyphs.

the activity of cosmic forces and the passage of time, a great mandala of rotary movement and immobility, evolution and involution, spiritual progress or regression.

The pole on which the Sun Dance Wheel is fixed represents the still center of the universe, Aristotle's "unmoved mover," the Taoist "sage" "chosen one," invisible at the center, who moves the Wheel without moving himself. René Guénon quotes the following Taoist passages: "The sage is he who has attained the central point of the Wheel and remains bound to the Unvarying Mean, in indissoluble union with the Origin, partaking of its immutability and imitating its non-acting activity." "He who has reached the highest degree of emptiness, will be secure in repose. To return to the root is to enter the state of repose," i.e. to throw off the bonds of transitory things.

The Wheel of Law, Truth and Life, is one of the eight emblems of good luck in Chinese Buddhism, showing the way of escape from the illusory world of rotation and from illusions, and the way towards the Center. Freemasons will remember that "point within a circle, round which a Mason cannot err." The teaching of the Circle is universal, and universally illustrated, from the child's spinning top to the great rose windows of the Gothic Cathedrals reflecting the Celestial Rose, beyond the limitations of time and space.

> "The Will rolled onward, like a Wheel
> In even motion, by the Love impelled,
> That moves the sun in Heaven and all the stars."
>
> Dante

The Sun Dance reflects the Cosmic Wheel in motion. The Dancers and the people at large believe that the yearly performance of the sacred ceremony, if properly performed, without mistakes, by dedicated men and women, will bless, not only the participants, their families and tribes, but the region, the country, the entire world. They believe that the Sun Dance is a sustaining force for good, blessed by the Great Spirit, conferring power and well-being on those who take part in it, to last them through the year.

The eight-day unfoldment of the Sun Dance is like a great solemn liturgical mass. The effect upon the "congregation," in the sense of the "gathered together," seems to be more direct and the outpouring of power more obvious, in proportion to the expenditure of human endeavor and dedication. The dancing is strenuous, the ordeal searching, as I have found the Indian way of fasting to be deeper, more fundamentally transforming than the Christian Churches' Lenten fast. The principle is the same. The Sun Dance is that sacred round which Gnostic tradition avers the Master Jesus danced with his disciples, the Dance of the Creation round and to the Creator, in which we, as created beings, also have our part.

Like the woman who lived in a square house, we can still be round house people. Though we may never paint our bodies with the sacred paint, nor wear the feathered regalia, nor join our brethren in Wyoming, Arizona, New Mexico, and other consecrated places, in the eight-day observance of the great renewal festival, yet we may, we should, we must, dance the Sun Dance daily in our hearts, if we would reach our own place on the Great Medicine Wheel.

PART THREE

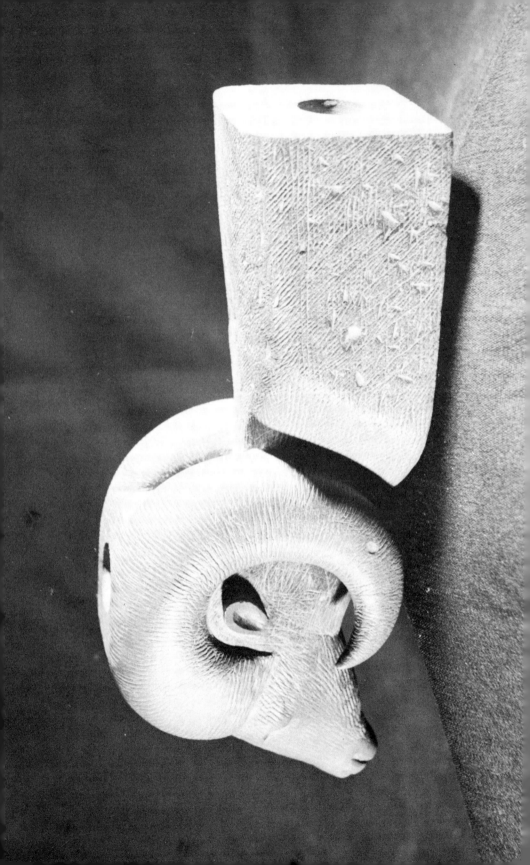

XIII

"Most people call it a 'peace pipe,' yet now there is no peace on earth or even between neighbors, and I have been told that it has been a long time since there has been peace in world." Black Elk.

"Behold this pipe! Always remember how sacred it is, and treat it as such, for it will take you to the end. With this pipe the two-leggeds will increase, and there will come to them all that is good. From above Wakan-Tanka has given to you this sacred pipe, so that through it you may have knowledge." The Sacred Buffalo Woman of the Lakota Sioux.

"O Wakan-Tanka, You are the truth. The two-legged peoples who put their mouths to this pipe will become the truth itself; there will be in them nothing impure. Help us to walk the sacred path of life without difficulty, with our minds and hearts continually fixed on You." High Hollow Horn.

The Sacred Pipe is the universal, essential channel between the Great Spirit and his children. There are many legends about how it first came to the different tribes. In the Arapaho version it was given to their ancestors at the beginning of the world, when the Turtle had brought the earth up from under the water. It was delivered to them by the Duck, who was swimming on the top of the water, after the land appeared. At the same time they were given an ear of corn, from which comes all the corn of the world.

The Turtle changed the Pipe to stone, and also the first Ear of Corn. The Pipe, the Turtle and the Ear of Corn are preserved among the northern Arapaho in Wyoming, handed down in the keeping of a particular family from generation to generation, carefully wrapped in deerskin. They are exposed only on rare occasions and always within a sacred tipi in the presence of a few holy men and carefully selected witnesses.

The Sioux have another version of the coming of the sacred Pipe.

99

Their legend is in the National Monument at Pipestone, Minnesota, where the red stone for the pipeheads of all tribes is still quarried as it was thousands of years ago, and still only by Indians.

This legend says that the Pipe was brought to the people by a Sacred White Buffalo Woman, who explained it to them, holding it up before them, stem first to the heavens.

"With this sacred Pipe you will walk upon the Earth, for the Earth is sacred. Every step taken upon her should be a prayer. The bowl of this pipe is of red stone. It is of the Earth. The stem of the pipe is of wood, and this represents all that grows upon the Earth. The feathers which hang where the stem fits into the bowl represent the Eagle and all the wingeds of the air. All things of the universe are joined to you who smoke the pipe, all send their voices to the Great Spirit. When you pray with this pipe, you pray for and with everything created."

The stem is sometimes used alone, in sacred dances, to bless objects, and in other ways, like the magician's baton or rod, which also must be fashioned of certain woods, gathered in a certain way, and then consecrated to its magical uses. A perfectly straight branch of almond or hazel cut before the tree blossomed, with a golden sickle, in early dawn, was one of the recommended methods of preparation. The almond or hazel should be "virgin, having no branches or off-shoots." It was also hollow, by implication, like the Chinese Hollow Bamboo, since one old manual says that "a needle (or long spike) of magnetized iron ran throughout."

The Chinese Hollow Bamboo represented the Sage or wise man after the pith of the lower self had been withdrawn. It referred to the Tao of right living, "sageliness within, kingliness without," its written character combined *shou* (head) with *ch'o* (foot), expressing wholeness, inner growth, and also step by step progress, a setting forth upon the way.

Sageliness or wisdom is an inner achievement. Kingliness refers to the ruler, in ancient days considered divine, and serving as the connecting link between Heaven and Earth, interpreting and transmitting the Way of Heaven to those on Earth, and the worship of those on Earth to Heaven. This is also the function of the Pipe, to be the two-way communication, the "pipeline" between the Great Spirit and His children.

In Wisecraft (witchcraft) "every stick or straight line embodies implications of direction and intensity," and the rod is used as a channel of universal power. The *Grand Grimoire* devotes a whole chapter to the composition of a mysterious wand, which could also be misused as a destroying or blasting rod. So also the Pipestem can be misused, as everything created for right use and enjoyment can be, and often is, misused. We need only think of Atomic Energy and other Twentieth-Century new and re-discoveries, to understand the symbol of the Blasting Rod.

The Bible frequently refers to rods of power. The rod of Moses destroyed the rods of the Egyptian priests, and gave victory to the Israelites. When Moses struck the rock with his rod, water gushed forth. Aaron and others had rods of power, and used them, but perhaps the most familiar reference to the rod is the psalmist's cry to the Lord, "Thy rod and Thy staff shall comfort me."

The rod has interesting derivatives, including the royal sceptre, the marshal's baton, the conductor's baton, the battle club, and the Tarot wand. Medical magicians used a rod during the performance of their cures and some "wise" doctors still do. A rod with entwined serpents is the symbol of the medical profession.

The rod is used in Alchemy, as the first of the four essential tools of magic, also represented in the four Tarot suits, the rod (or wand), the cup, the sword, the pentacle. It is the first of the four letters of the Divine Name, the Tetragrammaton. We find it in the Kaballah and in many other contexts, but this should be enough to indicate the meaning and the usage of the Pipestem.

The Pipehead is carved from red catlinite (pipestone) quarried chiefly at the Pipestone National Monument in Minnesota, where for centuries representatives of all the tribes journeyed to obtain the stone for their pipes. Permission to quarry, fashion, and sell pipestones within the monument has been reserved by law to American Indians, who still work in the pits in the late summer and fall, as their ancestors did.

The layer of pipestone is covered by Sioux quartzite, rough and granular, in contrast to the smooth, soapy-feeling pipestone. There was once a seashore here, where a deposit of muddy clay was buried in sand. Pressure, heat and chemical action changed the sand into quartzite and the clay into pipestone.

The color of the stone is significant. Red is the color of the earth, the color of blood, the color of the redskinned peoples. "The Morning Star is like a man; he is painted red all over; that is the color of life." (Pawnee chant.) Long before the rise of western civilizations, when the white man was still a barbarian, the civilized peoples of Northern Africa and Asia Minor, Egyptians and Aryans, considered themselves part of the red race and were proud to belong to it. Egyptians used henna to stain the bodies a deeper red, and painted an exaggerated shade of red on human forms in all their pictures.

Red is one of the four elements (fire), one of the four corners of the earth, the four directions (south), in China the Guardian of the South has a red face. "He holds the umbrella of chaos, at the elevation of which there is universal darkness, thunder and earthquake." The Thibetans give the color red to the west, instead of to the south, and there are other variations among people as remote from one another as Egypt and Ireland, but all are agreed that among the four elements, red is the color and has the significance of fire. To the American Indian red always symbolizes the day, as black symbolizes night. To the Cherokee red signifies success and triumph. In Alchemy the principal colors were black, white, gold and red, "symbolized by the Phoenix and extracted from white." "The deep redness of the Sun perfecteth the work of Sulphur, which is called the fire of the Stone, the King's Crown, the Son of Sol, wherein the first labor of the workman resteth."

Sophic Sulphur, or gold, was frequently called the Red King. One alchemist wrote, "Soon after your tincture shall have become heated in the Philosophic Egg, it becomes with wonderful appearances, blacker than the crow, afterwards, in succession of time, whiter than the swan; and at last passing through a yellow color, it turns out more red than any blood."

Red, the vigorous color of health, was the most interesting and frequently used color in magic healing. In music Scriabin gave the color red to the note C. Newton also gave the color red to the note C and the sound Do. Before Newton, astronomers writing of the music of the Spheres gave red to the Planet Mars, and the sound C-do.

There are many more aspects and analogies to be found in the color of the sacred pipestone. In passing one might notice the Red Lion which converts metal into gold, a byproduct of the Philosopher's Stone; the Red Cap the witches of Ireland put on to fly to their sacred meeting places, and the symbolism of crossing the Red Sea, the most dangerous part of an undertaking, or of a stage in life. To leave Egypt for the Promised Land implied the crossing of this Red Sea, a symbol of spiritual evolution, purification by fire, and also of death seen as the threshold between worlds of matter and of spirit.

Whenever the pipehead is joined to the pipestem, for the purpose of sacred smoking, all these elements are present. The tobacco stands for the vegetable world and the ascending smoke, combining the elements of air and fire, as the pipehead (clay) combines those of earth and water, is the symbol of the relationship between earth and heaven, the path through fire to transmutation. According to Geber, the alchemist, smoke symbolizes the soul leaving the body. There are also folklore traditions which assert that a beneficent power in the smoke can protect people, animals and plants from misfortune.

So that when a man takes his pipe (or a woman hers, because among Paiutes and some other tribes women may have the pipe,) and goes into the desert or upon the mountain, or along a stream in the foothills, somewhere quiet and perhaps still unpolluted, to sit in a sacred manner and smoke in the ancient way, there is set up a communication channel between the all and the ALL, "a hot line to Heaven," a pipeline through which messages and signals ascend and descend.

In dangerous moments, when there is not time for ritual preparation, to hold the Pipe and lift it and the spirit upward, brings protection and help. There are many other ways in which the power of the Pipe works infallibly, but these belong to those who have earned the right to use them.

"I am sorrowful," an old chief said, "I have given my white brother my tobacco, and he is using it to kill himself."

A pipe, even a cigarette, should be smoked in the right way, first puff to the Great Holy, second puff to Mother Earth, third, fourth, fifth, sixth puffs to the four Great Powers of the Four Directions, giving thanks for all the blessings of this life. After that each puff a prayer, including one puff for each person present as you smoke. In that way, used in prayer, the tobacco will not harm one, or if it does injure the human overcoat, heart and spirit will be purified, and those present receive a blessing.

The same holds true for wine, for those who cannot give up alcohol — first sip to the Great Mystery, second sip to Mother Earth, the next four to the Four Great Powers, and after that, each sip a thanksgiving or a prayer, not forgetting a sip for each of those present. The results can be astonishing.

XIV

FAR FROM OWENS VALLEY and the rock drawings at Coso, the same symbols are found, circles, ladders, shields, medicine bags and sacred animals, incised in stone, in the forests, by the inland lakes, and on the seashore, in Nova Scotia and New Brunswick where my grandfather's Algonkian people lived and where their scattered descendants struggle to live today.

Louis Mitchell, a Passamaquoddy who had been in the Legislature in Maine, "collected and wrote out with the strictest literalness a great number of manuscripts." These were translated by Charles Godfrey Leland and John D. Prince, in their book: *Kuluskap The Master and Other Algonkian Poems*. Funk & Wagnells, New York, 1902, the year that I was born.

I heard these legends as a child, and was taken to Cape Blomidon to see where Glooscap (Kuluskap) was supposed to live. One of them, *Nilun pesazmuk elintaquik*, The Song of the Stars, reminds me of Paiute songs and stories.

> *The Song of the Stars*
> We are the stars which sing
> We sing with our light.
> We are the birds of fire
> We fly across the heaven,
> Our light is a star.
> We make a road for Spirits,
> A road for the Great Spirit.
> Among us are three hunters
> Who chase a bear.
> There never was a time
> When they were not hunting;
> We look down on the mountains,
> This is the song of the mountains.

Another, *What Kuluskap did for the Indians*, is the story of Creation and of the journey toward the Great Spirit where "whoever went to seek him, the Master ever found."

In the very olden time
Before Kuluskap the Master
The Lord of beasts and men
Had come into the world,
Or man was by him instructed,
All lived in wonderful darkness;
Men could not even see
To slay their enemies,
But the Lord brought light unto them,
The daybreak and the dawn.
Therefore for this his people
Are known as the Wabenaki
The men of the Early Dawn.
And many a thing he taught them,
Showed them the hidden virtues
Of plants and roots and blossoms.
And all the herbs which Indians
Could use for any purpose,
And also every creature,
Beasts, birds and all the fishes,
All things which could be eaten
Or serve for joy to man.

Then pointing to the heaven,
He taught the names of the stars
And all the wonderful stories,
The very old traditions
Of all that the planets had been.

107

"We make a road for Spirits. A road for
the Great Spirit."

He greatly loved mankind
And wherever he might be,
Though afar in the wilderness
He was never far away,
Away from his Indian children.
He dwelt in a lonely land,
But whoever went to seek him
The Master ever found.

That is the quest, the journey, the human pilgrimage.

Mary Austin, author and friend of many Indians, who lived in Owens Valley, near the place where I live now, aware of the approaching day when Snowy Earth Comes Gliding, wrote this *Morning Prayer:*

I arise, facing East,
I am asking toward the light;
I am asking that my day
Shall be beautiful with light.
I am asking that the place
Where my feet are shall be light,
That as far as I can see
I shall follow it aright.
I am asking for the courage
To go forward through the shadow,
I am asking toward the light!

OTHER BOOKS BY EVELYN EATON

I Send A Voice
Quietly My Captain Waits
and other historical novels
Flight
Go Ask the River
The Trees and Fields Went the Other Way

BOOKS FROM THE BEAR TRIBE

The Path Of Power, by Sun Bear, continues to interpret ancient philosophies for today's readers. In the *Path Of Power*, readers will learn:
How to seek and find vision in their lives
How to find and follow their own path of power
Why their path of power is the reason for their being alive on this planet at this time.
Over 100,000 copies sold. Now in its third printing from Prentice Hall.
$9.95 pb (add $2.00 P&H)

The Bear Tribe's Self–Reliance Book, by Sun Bear, Wabun, Nimimosha and the Tribe. New & Revised. A guide for everyone interested in returning to the land. It contains basic skills for re–establishing a proper relationship with the land and all beings upon it, as well as Native American and New Age philosophies, prophecies and visions.
$9.95 pb (add $2.00 P&H)

Walk In Balance, the companion volume to *The Bear Tribe's Self–Reliance Book*. See ad on following page.

The Book Of The Vision Quest, by Steven Foster and Meredith Little, is an absorbing account of the personal transformation which takes place in the Native tradition of vision questing. The authors have guided hundreds of people through the intense experience of seeking vision and explain the steps involved.
$9.95 pb (add $2.00 P&H)

The Medicine Wheel: Earth Astrology, by Sun Bear and Wabun. A system of earth astrology to help guide people not only in their daily lives, but in their life path as well. The book combines Native legends, lore and wisdom, with the vision of Sun Bear to help the reader walk in balance on the Earth Mother.
Over 500,000 copies sold worldwide.
$9.95 pb (add $2.00 P&H)

Woman Of The Dawn, by Wabun Wind. An unprecedented behind–the–scenes look into the early days of the Bear Tribe, and a very human portrait of Sun Bear. Wabun retraces her steps along the path of inner discovery from succesful New York writer to medicine helper to Sun Bear.
$18.95 hc (add $2.00 P&H)

Lightseeds, by Wabun Wind and Anderson Reed. One of the most comprehensive books on crystals now available. With techniques ranging from the basic to the advanced, this book appeals to the novice enthusiast as well as the experienced practitioner.
$8.95 pb (add $2.00 P&H)

ORDER FROM:
Bear Tribe Publishing • PO Box 9167 • Spokane, WA 99209
Send 1.00 for catalog

BEAR TRIBE PUBLISHING
Videos

Sun Bear: On Power

"Your Path Of Power is your reason for being alive on the planet at this time. In past generations, people knew how to find and follow their path of power. Today we have been taught to give our power away to a society that often misuses it."
— **Sun Bear**

Find out how to gain power in your life, and put it to work for you.

Sun Bear: Earth Changes

"The Earth Changes prophesied by many Native Traditions have already begun. People need look no further than the daily news to see proof of this. The people who are going to survive the changes are people who can walk in a sacred manner, who live in harmony with each other and the Earth."
— **Sun Bear**

From his unique and varied experiences, Sun Bear discusses Earth Changes and how they will affect you.

Wabun Wind: The Feminine

"People are afraid to look at the wholeness of who they are and part of the reason they are afraid is because of history. The Patriarchal society teaches us to be in our heads. The rest is to be disregarded. The emotions, are frightening. We are taught not to feel. If we feel, we can't be logical. If we feel, we don't fit into society. This is a very sad thing."
— **Wabun Wind**

Learning to revalue the feminine is a critical part of coming back into balance.

VHS or Beta
65 minutes each
$24.95
(add $2.00 P&H)

Order From:
Bear Tribe Publishing • PO Box 9167 • Spokane, WA 99209

True balance begins with you!